Walking
on and around
The Cotswold Way

David Hunter

Published by Sigma Leisure – an imprint of Sigma Press, 1 South Oak Lane, Wilmslow, Cheshire SK9 6AR, England.

British Library Cataloguing in Publication Data
A CIP record for this book is available from the British Library.

ISBN: 1-85058-483-4

Typesetting and design by: Sigma Press, Wilmslow, Cheshire.

Cover design: The Agency, Wilmslow, Cheshire

Cover photograph: On The Cotswold Way, Wood Stanley.

Photography: David & Vera Hunter

Maps: Vera Hunter

Printed by: MFP Design and Print

Also by David Hunter: Walking The Brecon Beacons and The Black Mountains *(Sigma Leisure)*

Preface

Walking a long distance footpath is an attractive prospect but not always a practical one. Constraints of time, family commitments or physical considerations may make it a dream that can never be realised. But circular walks along the route in short sections can be both acceptable and preferable, since you can choose the time, the place and the pace. The Cotswold Way lends itself admirably to this approach, affording all the pleasures of a day in the open air, which is both rewarding and mentally renewing.

This justly-famous countryside is within reasonable access of large centres of population and extends an invitation that is hard to resist, for all ages and abilities. By following the suggested routes you will, at your own convenience and with weather of your choosing, have explored much of the best that the Way has to offer.

The book also offers some ideas for linking routes. It tells something of the history of the region and suggests places of interest to visit on or near the Way. It does not, however, provide a step by step guide to the Cotswold Way nor does it cover its whole length.

Caution

While care has been taken in compiling this book, footpaths may be subject to change with permanent or temporary diversions. It is quite impossible for any map or guidebook to keep fully up to date, so be prepared to make amendments to the suggested routes. Neither the author nor the publisher can accept any responsibility for damage or injury howsoever caused. Motorists are advised to securely lock their cars and to avoid leaving valuables on display.

David Hunter

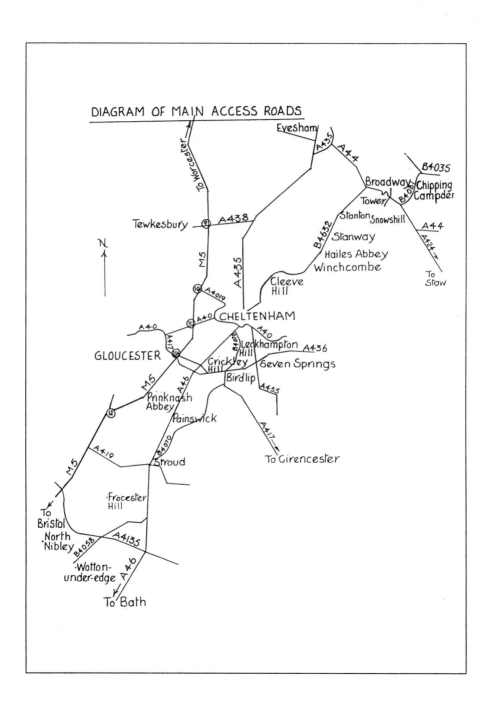

DIAGRAM OF MAIN ACCESS ROADS

Contents

Introduction

Conclusion

First Steps

The Cotswold Way follows the western edge of the hills. In the course of its hundred-mile journey from Chipping Campden southward to Bath it rides the hill tops and dips down to the towns and villages. At times you will be lifted high on a sharp-edged scarp, exultant with the wide views, your horizon limited only by the bounds of nature and your own imagination. Within minutes you may be picking your way along the narrow confines of a path that runs through growing crops, waist-high in ripening barley; or following a well-used bridleway decorated with wild flowers now fugitive from the fields created by modern farming practice. In less than a mile you will have plunged into the anonymity of the woodland, serenaded by its vocal but often elusive inhabitants. Onward then to a quiet village, where you may find refreshment or stop to enjoy the peace and tranquillity within the walls of its ancient church. All that within the space of a day's walking!

The hills and valleys have long been the home of man and he has left his imprint on the landscape in many ways. The pattern of the fields and hedgerows may tell a story, pre-historic tracks, Roman roads and saltways add their testimony. Much of the history of the villages may be written on the walls of its churches or in the parish registers. Our more distant ancestors living in the hill top camps so often encountered along the way, also gave thought to the next life honouring their dead in barrows like Belas Knap. The map is dotted with references to the villas of the Romans who lived in rather more comfort with their underfloor heating and mosaic tiling. There are families living in everyday circumstances, whose forebears are remembered for only a generation or two, and others in great houses, their walls covered with portraits of the past: the good, the bad and the ugly of half a millennium. Bookmarks in the pages of history that we can read for ourselves and complicated, incomplete jigsaws for which we rely upon the interpretation of the archaeologist.

The old roads and tracks have seen the passage of many men,

priests, pilgrims, and princes. Men-at-arms have passed this way: tinkers, traders, cattle drovers, adventurers, charlatans. Some travelling to fulfil their responsibilities, others running away from them.

To all these is added today's walker, who is here simply for the pleasure it affords. A pleasure to be enjoyed at many levels, whether simply being out in the open air or enriched by the enjoyment of some particular interest: photography, sketching, bird-watching, identifying wild flowers, exploring the little villages and local museums. Some will take the Way at a fast pace, others may prefer a more leisured progress with time to sit upon the top of a hill and watch the clouds roll by.

Whatever it is that you may need, – exercise of mind or body, respite from the cares of the week, the stimulation of new surroundings, a pleasant family outing or the peace of solitude – you should find in it and around the gentle Cotswold Hills.

Cotswold Way sign on Fish Hill, Broadway

Practical Matters

Maps

A map is always a good investment for a walker and the relevant sheet number of the Ordnance Survey map is given at the start of each walk. You are strongly recommended to carry a map with you. Apart from the obvious use of finding the way, it provides a wealth of interesting detail not directly related to navigation. A map, even when following a published route, is a useful tool in several respects. It should quickly resolve any problems in the interpretation of text and put you back on course if you have missed a turning. It allows for changes of route, extending or cutting short a walk to suit the prevailing conditions. Checking the destinations of interesting-looking crossing paths will often help plan future walks, and sitting on a hilltop on a summer's day, spotting distant features of the landscape, is a rewarding occupation.

Maps might be the walker's Bible but should not always be relied upon to tell the complete truth. They can never be totally up to date, footpaths are subject to diversions (sometimes temporary) which can take the map makers some time to amend.

Paths and Bridleways

Paths writ large on the map may not be so clearly defined on the ground and in some cases may disappear altogether. There are several reasons for this. Footpath diversions have already been mentioned. It's boots that make paths and under-use, sometimes coupled with the rapid summer growth of vegetation, may leave room for uncertainty. If this sort of path is given up then it may well disappear from use altogether; so the walker should learn to take the rough with the smooth and play a part in keeping the footpath network intact. Footpaths that cross arable land can disappear at ploughing time, especially if they cross a field rather than following the hedgerow. Some farmers carefully leave the path alone, no doubt reckoning that in the end it causes less disturbance. Others plough through but sometimes fail to reinstate them as required and it may be left to the boots of pioneering walkers to recover the lost way. Some footpaths over fields of growing crops may have been replaced by locally used and acceptable alternatives. These do not necessarily appear on maps and yet are obviously well used, but here take care to ensure that you are not trespassing.

Don't be put off by these words of caution. Intelligent use of the map will solve most problems.

Waymarking and Signposting

Almost all public footpaths and bridleways in the area are sign-posted at the point where they leave the road, often with a destination and distance indicated. Thereafter you may need to rely on your map reading, although there is often additional waymarking, you cannot expect to find this on every route.

Waymarks where in place are found on walls, gates, stiles, tree trunks and sometimes on posts where a path may cross a large field. Waymark coding is as follows:

Footpaths   yellow arrows

Bridleways   blue arrows

By-ways   red arrows

Other symbols may be used in conjunction with these – long distance paths under the aegis of the Countryside Commission are marked with a white acorn or circular routes with the letters CR. These are general indicators. The Cotswold Way is waymarked by a white spot, sometimes within one of the coloured arrows. It is also very clearly signed where the path leaves or crosses a road. Generally it represents one of the best examples of waymarking that I know for its clarity and consistency. The long anticipated official adoption of the Cotswold Way as a National Trail will eventually add the acorn logo to the signing.

What to Wear

Vast acres of paper have been covered with advice to walkers on what to wear in all given circumstances, for our purpose common sense should prevail.

Aim to be comfortable at all times. Layer of clothing easily put on and off is the secret of temperature control. Invest in a good, medium sized rucksack which will carry all your needs for the day, leaving your hands free to operate a camera, binoculars or for map reading. Your rucksack should be comfortable to wear, with broad shoulder straps properly adjusted. If you are not confident of its waterproof qualities, use a bin liner. Apart from food and drink, you should carry spare clothing, i.e. waterproof jacket and leggings, extra pull-over, gloves and a first aid kit. Hats are important: a woolly bobble hat to defeat the cold or something to provide protection from the sun. Basic standard wear is a matter for the individual but my preference is for knee breeches or shorts, light or heavyweight shirts according to season and as many secure pockets as possible. Body warmers are excellent and allow for extra pockets to be stitched into the inside of the garment. There are also some very useful light-weight trousers available, with a generous collection of pockets, which are a good alternative to shorts.

Just as much paper has been ink-blackened in the cause of proclaiming the rival merits of footwear. Stout shoes or even trainers are often practical, wellies are out for distance walking but for real comfort you can't beat the support provide by a good, but not necessarily expensive, pair of boots. You should look for padded ankle tops, sewn-in tongues and good sole grip. Despite the diffi-culty there may be in fully waterproofing some lightweight boots I opt for these whenever possible, reserving medium weight leather boots, regularly treated with Nikwax, for winter or bad weather walking. Socks too are important, they may seem expensive but a good brand of walking sock will greatly add to your foot comfort and should last many years.

Small Children

Toddlers and young babes are sometimes to be seen in papoose carriers. These are excellent, but remember that while the exercise may be keeping you nice and warm the passive child can become quite cold and cases of hypothermia are not unknown.

When to Walk

The Cotwolds offer good all year round walking, each season bringing its own particular interest, the fresh greening of spring, the wild flowers and ripening harvest of high summer. The golden days of autumn give way to the delights of brisk winter walking, over frost hardened ground with the sometimes added enchantment of a light scattering of snow on the hills.

Walk 1: Speedwell

Chipping Campden and circuit to Broadway

Route: Chipping Campden — Dovers Hill — Broadway Tower — Broadway — Saintbury — Chipping Campden

Map: 1:50,000 Landranger sheets 150 and 151, 1:25,000 Pathfinder 1043 (SP03/13)

Distance: 11 miles

Parking: Chipping Campden (limited) Fish Hill, Broadway

Toilets: Chipping Campden, Fish Hill, Broadway

Picnic site: Fish Hill

Chipping Campden

Chipping Campden is famed far beyond the Cotswolds and far beyond these islands. The visitor, arriving here for the first time, knows exactly what he expects to see, for nearly every book about Britain has a photograph of the church or market hall and often both. Calendar publishers, with the picturesque wealth of the nation to draw upon, are happy to brighten the year with images of the village. Guide books, with a thousand places to be fitted within the covers, devote pages rather than paragraphs, to sing its praises. And well they might, for here is today's vision of the past, for some, the perfect English village in a perfect setting.

Its past and present prosperity is reflected in the quality of its buildings. There is a long tradition of craftsmanship proudly continued today, well-exampled by the care taken in the maintenance and restoration work which is so vital to the preservation of our architectural heritage. The town's location, in perfect sheep country, gave it centuries of stability at a time when the wealth of the country was measured in wool rather than in gold bullion. Many places recall their past with street names and Campden is no exception, witness Sheep Street and Dyers Lane.

The buildings have their origins in several different centuries but dwell together in great harmony. Fortunately they were unaffected by the Industrial Revolution which imposed so much ugliness elsewhere, in the struggle to compete in expanding mass production markets. No dark satanic mills sprang up to cast their shadows upon Campden's golden stones or blacken its skies. When the new age was ushered in Campden went into a forced retirement as lack of the necessary power source, water, moved the wool processing elsewhere.

The breadth of its streets is a reminder that the town has a long history as a market. Sir Baptist Hicks, the first Viscount Campden, had the many-arched market hall built in 1627 to aid the sale of local produce. The National Trust, present owners of the hall, has re-roofed the building and restored the family arms. The Woolstaplers Hall, now a venerable six hundred years old, houses the local museum and the Tourist Information Office, a modern industry in the home of yesterdays.

Notwithstanding the wealth of its secular buildings, it is the parish church of St. James that provides the abiding memory. Bathed in the warming light of a spring day, this fine example of a wool church is as handsome as many a cathedral, with its graceful 120 feet high tower dominant. Within all is brightness, the light flooding through the clerestory windows forbidding the gloom that is a feature of some churches. I leave readers to explore the church for themselves, to discover, amongst many other things, the huge brass memorial, eight feet by four, to the flower of the wool merchants of all England, William Grevel. No less spectacular is the tomb where Sir Baptist and Lady Hicks lie in state under a canopy, supported by black marble columns.

Memorial inscriptions are not always easy to read but patience often reveals some little gems, such as this to Lady Penelope Noel:

"Most exquisite model of nature's best workmanship
The richest magazine of all divine and moral virtues

St James' Parish Church

Penelope Opie Noel
Having added to the dignity of her birth a brighter shine of true
nobleness
Example sweetness of her conversation, her contempt of earthly
vanities
And her zealous affection towards heaven. After 22 years devotions
commended her virgin soul into the hands of its true bridegroom,
Jesus Christ, May 17th AD 1633, over whose precious dust, here
preserved,
Her sad parent Edward Noel, Viscount Campden and the Lady Lilian
his Wife dropped their tears and erected this marble to the dear
memories
Of their invaluable loss."

There must have been a special talent in composing such epitaphs
– certainly they don't write them like that any more. Lady Penelope's
early demise has echoes of a fairy story, but without the happy
ending, for she pricked her finger while sewing and died from the
resultant blood poisoning. This is becoming a little too sombre we
must be on our way.

It is an interesting thought, in these less religious days, that we
start from the steps of one church with the Cotswold Way terminat-
ing at another, for the walker reaches journeys end beneath the steps
of the Jacob's ladder that graces the west front of Bath Abbey. There
would have been a time when a traveller might have been glad to
have sought the blessing of the Church before setting out on a
journey, and have hastened to give thanks for safe arrival.

A guard of honour, the twelve apostles no less, sends the walker
on his way. If that seems a little fanciful, it should be explained that
the reference is to the pollarded lime trees that edge the church path.
The gate-house on the left is that of Campden House, once the
splendid home of the enormously wealthy merchant, Sir Baptist
Hicks. The mansion was one of the many casualties, both people
and property, of the bitter Civil War that divided the country when
King and Parliament were in conflict. A long chain of events sparked
off when, in January, 1642, Charles I took an armed party to the
House of Commons in a bid to arrest five of its members. Campden
House was destroyed, not by direct assault, but by the scorched earth

policy of the Royalists, who put it to the torch to prevent the Parliamentarians making use of it. Another version suggests the fire resulted from the drunken behaviour of the retreating Cavaliers. If this was the truth of the matter, it is not difficult to see the propaganda value of the camouflage provided by the first story. Such things have a way of getting into the history books leaving the casual reader wondering exactly what did happen, but inclined to think the worst.

The row of alms houses opposite was the gift of Sir Baptist Hicks, one of many to church and village.

The Walk

On reaching the main street turn left and walk through the village, passing the Woolstaplers Hall and the Market Hall to reach Hoo Lane on the right. Here take the signposted Cotswold Way passing the neatly thatched St. Peter's Cottage its roofing matched by the bird table in the topiaried garden. Soon the lane narrows and steepens, leaving the houses behind.

The Cotswold Way is to be followed to Broadway. So, keeping an eye open for the waymarking, you can pretty well forget the map after a brief scan and settle down to enjoy the walk. Views are opening up, with Chipping Campden, snug within its encircling hills .

The path is edged with hawthorn, when in flower bringing back the argument concerning the old adage: "Ne'er cast a clout 'till May is out" . . . is it the flower or the month? Either way it never did seem particularly good advice. Pink campion challenges for a place among the wayside nettles and comfrey. Comfrey likes damp spots, where it sometimes grows in great abundance, producing bell-like flowers in white and shades of mauve and pink. Parts of the plant were once used as a salve for the treatment of cuts and sores.

In just over half a mile a road is reached (Kingcomb Lane) turn left and in about 150 yards take the path on the right signposted Dovers Hill. Here speedwell may be seen, a tiny blue flower with a white centre, surely a good omen for the walker. Away to the west is Broadway Tower, the end of the first leg of this walk.

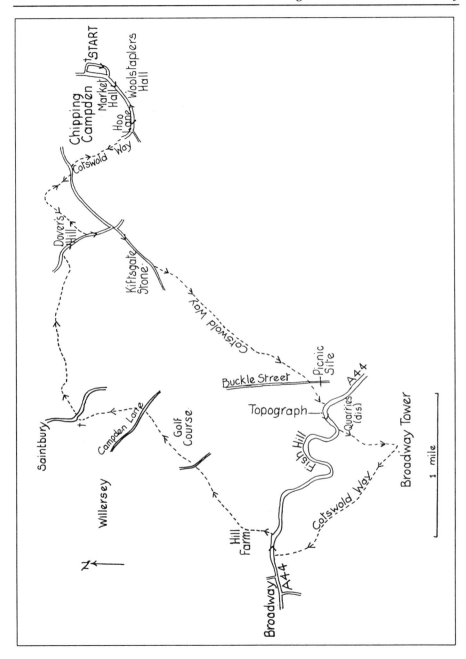

Cross the stile at the end of the field giving on to Dovers Hill. The path runs left along the hedgerow but go forward beyond the triangulation point to take in the view before continuing.

Dovers Hill

Here is a natural amphitheatre, looking out over Lynches Wood and the vale beyond with Aston Subedge below. The fields present an irregular chequer board effect, not in black and white but in green and perhaps the yellow of oilseed rape. One year there were a dozen blocks of this colourful crop in an erratic pattern. Perhaps the NFU might be persuaded to organise its members to plant in a more regular manner so that the hilltop viewer might enjoy the visual effect of a landscaped chess board. A foolish fantasy, but stranger things have been done, like the man whom a few years ago installed a vast curtain across a Californian desert.

The hill is named after a colourful character, Captain Robert Dover, a lawyer by profession and a bit of a wag by inclination. It was he, who having obtained the support of James I started the Cotswold Olympick Games on this site in 1612. The event seems to have been extremely popular for it continued for 240 years when increasing disorderly behaviour brought it to an end, subsequently to be revived in the Festival of Britain year, 1951.

Not all the competition activities could be expected to feature in the modern Olympics and so far as I know there are no plans to introduce gold medals for shin kicking, hare-coursing or cock-fighting. Some of the other events would still qualify, like wrestling, jumping and throwing the hammer. In a measure the games were not unlike medieval jousting, but perhaps a little short on the knightly courtesies, with Dover riding forth from a mock battle to set the games in motion with bugle blast and canon's roar.

It is not only the lively Captain Dover that is remembered here. A topograph has been erected to mark the efforts of Benjamin Chandler and Frederick Griggs, who helped acquire this windy hilltop for the National Trust in 1926. The inscribed plate points the way to Edge Hill – 15 miles, Brown Clee Hill – 44 miles, The Long Mynd – 56 miles, Clee Hill – 41 miles and many other points of the compass. A wealth of walking possibilities for future exploration but a modest topography compared with the expansionist thinking of the designer of its rival which we shall encounter on Fish Hill.

Leave Dovers Hill by the small car park, turn left along the lane to reach the crossroad in just over 200 yards. Here turn right, and in 300 yards pass the Kiftsgate Stone set back off the road on your right.

Kiftsgate Stone

Visually this is not in the same league as the impressive stone monuments that attract the tourists' attention. Barely three feet high, moss covered, with a hole just off centre and brightened at its base with a little clump of celandines. Not very exciting to look at and yet of sufficient importance for the Ordnance Survey to include upon its maps. It is said to have been a meeting place of the Hundred, a mark stone on an ancient road, and up to 1738 the spot where the proclamation of the accession of the monarch took place. Alfred Watkins makes a mention of it in his controversial book "The Old Straight Track." It was he who propounded the theory of ley lines, in essence that the ancient tracks that crisscross the country were surveyed rather than occurring in haphazard fashion. The book is filled with references to sun alignments, mark stones, mounds, monuments and sight notches; fascinating reading however superficial your interest.

Continue with the road for a further two hundred yards then join the path on the left. Pursue this over the fields until Buckle Street is crossed, in a little over a mile and a quarter. The path gives some views of the valley below in which the new Campden House stands. Buckle Street, is another old track, its modern name derived from an old word meaning a hill top route. Continue with the path to meet the busy A44 at the top of the oddly named Fish Hill.

There is an excellent picnic site here, with car parking, toilets and information board which offers a suggestion of the origins of the Fish Hill name. Topographs are a popular feature of the Cotswold hills and this one does not confine itself to the observable points of the landscape. Broadway is nearest at a mile, but the traveller (hopefully not on foot) is also pointed to Edinburgh and John O' Groats. As we know all roads lead to Rome and from Fish Hill this is just 1306 miles. The compilers are nothing if not enthusiastic and in case we are about to set off to New York, they tell us it is but 3370 miles distant. Even this is not the limit of their horizon and they excel themselves with Sydney, 10950 miles. It was about this time that I started looking for directions to Mars and the Moon . . .

Cross the main road and take the Cotswold Way through a short wooded stretch and then into the open, passing old and long-disused quarries. Soon the turreted Broadway Tower comes into view. A welcome landmark, just as the medieval traveller would have been pleased, not to say relieved, to have the first glimpse of his lord's standard fluttering over his castle.

The now undisturbed banks of the quarry are, in season, covered with the once common cowslip and early purple orchid. It is always a pleasure to discover an orchid and there are several varieties to be seen along the Way.

Cross into the grounds of the privately owned Country Park by the tower (more about this in the next walk) and turn right to make the long waymarked descent of a mile and a quarter into Broadway, enjoying the views as you go. Long-horned cattle may be seen in the fields around the tower.

The Cotswold Way is abandoned at Broadway (the town is featured in the next chapter). Emerging from the path into the main street, turn right and in about 300 yards take the path on the left signed to Willersey and Saintbury Church. Remember that now the waymarking will be by means of blue or yellow arrows.

In three hundred yards, at the end of an orchard and just short of Hill Farm, bear right uphill passing through three gates in quick succession. Follow the waymarked bridle path north easterly for a mile to Campden Lane. The path rises steadily and gives good retrospective views. En route a metalled track is reached and crossed. Then the path follows the edge of a breezy hill top with a golf course on the right and views over the Vale of Evesham. ·· ··

When Campden Lane is reached, ascend the bank opposite and follow the yellow arrowed route to Saintbury. Soon the topmost tip of St. Nicholas's church peeps over the hill, the rest hidden beyond the sharp slopes. After crossing a stile, make the steep descent into the churchyard.

Saintbury Church

The saintly bishop is at the door to welcome the visitor, a carving depicts him with a ship in full sail cradled in his arm. He was the origin of our Santa Claus and many legends have been associated with him. He is credited with preventing a shipwreck by setting fire to trees on a cliff top at the height of a storm (the illuminated Christmas tree!) and so becoming the patron saint of sailors. In St. Nicholas's church at Abingdon (Oxfordshire), there is a window depicting the Bishop rescuing three boys from a brine barrel. One version of the story claims that the lads had been murdered and Nicholas miraculously restored them to life.

It is cool within the church, with its box pews and barrel-vaulted roof. Numbered among the long list of rectors dating from 1301 is William Latymer. He was a scholarly man, a fellow of All Souls and tutor to Reginald Pole who later became Archbishop of Canterbury.

Follow the church path to the road, turn right and in a few yards join the waymarked path on the left. In about a quarter of a mile the path changes direction from north-east to south-east for about 100 yards, then heads eastwards. Ignore the north-south crossing paths and tracks to reach a road just a little north of Dovers Hill, having travelled about a mile and a quarter from Saintbury. Turn right and in about a quarter of a mile turn left on to Dovers Hill and retrace your outward route to Chipping Campden.

Walk 2: To The Tower!

Broadway and its ancient church

Route: Broadway – Old Church – Broadway Tower – Broadway

Map: 1:50,000 Landranger 150, 1:25,000 Pathfinder 1043 (SP03/13)

Distance: 4 miles

Parking & Toilets: Leamington Road, Broadway

Broadway

The charms of Broadway have ensured it a place on the tourist trail and there is scarcely a time when it is not busy with visitors. Some making a quick exploration before their coach moves on, others, more in charge of their own itinerary, making a leisurely perambulation.

Sitting beneath the high Cotswold plateau, Broadway can be thought of as one of the gateways to the Vale of Evesham. It is not far beyond the town that the wayside fruit and vegetable stalls begin to appear. Soon the traveller is in the heart of that new farming industry – Pick your own – an invitation that is hard to resist, especially when strawberries are in season.

The visitor's Broadway is featured in its main street, unhappily also the busy A44, it has long needed a by-pass but it is difficult to see how this could be accomplished. The call for a by-pass may be a heartfelt appeal but forgets that the village grew up along a route in use for many centuries. It was a stopping place on one of the important drove roads out of Wales. Indeed it was a junction, with the Welsh drovers bringing in cattle via Worcester and Evesham, or from Hereford, Ledbury and Upton upon Severn. Cattle moved at a slow pace, following wide tracks, grazing as they went. In this context the very name Broadway takes on a new meaning. The inns that once catered for the drovers, a skilled and respectable occupation, found new patrons, refreshing travellers on the stage coach routes, and today, the modern tourist. Where once the Welsh cattle made their lugubrious way through the broad street, cars, not carts, clutter the town.

There is little, if any, reference in the usual guide books to the drovers, their pages deal with the more romantic discovery of the village by painters and writers. Not that they should be forgotten, for talented people like William Morris, Sir Edward Burne-Jones and the man who was both poet and painter, Dante Rossetti, spent time here.

Today's Broadway is a show place, attracting many tourists to its long street of mellowed stone. Its always clean and tidy, well-gardened, with no shortage of shops full of quality items of books, furniture and clothing, a browsers' delight.

The collector of sights, not handicapped by the constraints of storage, will find many little snippets to add to his impressions. On a sign above St. Patrick's Rooms, the saint is seen expelling snakes from Ireland. There are wisteria covered cottages close to the Swan Inn. A clock erected to commemorate Queen Victoria's Jubilee in 1887, was renovated to mark the second Elizabeth's coronation in 1953. There is an old milestone inscribed "This milestone was defaced under the defence regulations in 1939. Restored by public subscription to celebrate the coronation of Elizabeth II, June 1953." Clearly the ravages of war take a long time to heal.

Trees line the streets, at their very best in May when the pink candled chestnuts are in bloom. At Christmas, these trees are hung with lights and at this time Broadway looks its finest. Many a time I have driven from London on a winter's evening through the darkness of the winding roads from Stow to descend to the welcoming lights. The brightly lit shop windows and soft glow from behind closed curtains combining to give the now quiet village a peace and magic entirely appropriate to the season.

Broadway's famous Tower

The Walk

Leave the Leamington Road car park and turn left, on reaching the main street, turn right. In about 100 yards, opposite the Horse and Hounds Inn, take the path on the left signed to Old Church. It is a pleasant, waymarked path through the fields with sheep in lush green meadows. These Cotswold sheep live richly compared with some of their kin on the Welsh hills or the high fells of the Lake District who have to work so much harder for their living.

The Snowshill Road is met in just over half a mile, by Lybrook Farm. Here turn left to pass the wisteria covered, mellowed stone walls of the Court.

Charles I was entertained at Broadway Court in June 1644 during the dark days of the Civil War. With the conflict in its third year, he may have realised that his chances of victory were becoming slimmer. The end of June, however, gave him encouragement with a successful action at Cropredy Bridge near Banbury.

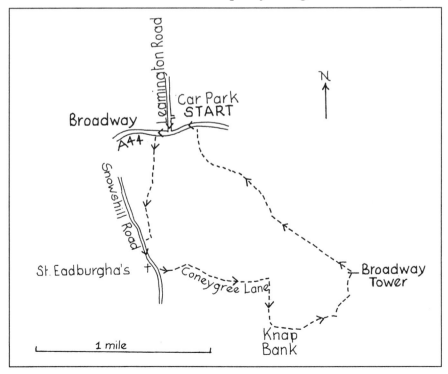

St. Eadburgha's Church

This ancient church, now redundant, but fortunately still open to visitors in the summer months, is full of interest. The continuing development of Broadway along the main road led to a shift of the population. Thus a new church replaced that of St. Eadburgha which had served the community from the beginning of the thirteenth century.

When Broadway celebrated its millennium in 1972 it was thought appropriate to place the commemorative stone within the old church.

There are not many churches that carry the name of Eadburgha, so she must be properly introduced. Eadburgha was in charge of a religious house founded by her grandmother in Winchester, at a time when that city was still capital of England. If the saint, until now, has been an unfamiliar figure, perhaps you are better acquainted with her royal grandfather, Alfred the Great.

The church has several features of interest. The bells are rung directly from the chancel floor, which sounds inconvenient. The ringing chamber was originally above the chancel in the central tower, but when the floor was removed for essential repairs so much light was let into the church it was decided not to replace it.

By the fourteenth century pulpit, is a pillar collecting box of about the same age. It is equipped with three locks, with a key for each of the church wardens and one for the vicar. Not exactly a trusting arrangement for such a place but it seems to have been standard practice for such boxes are to be seen elsewhere. Over the tower arch can be seen the Arms of Charles I. It was usual for the sovereign's heraldry to be displayed in churches, but not common to find Charles so represented. It poses a question: did some royalist supporter consider it expedient to conceal the coat of arms and replace it later?

You expect to find memorials remembering the departed in churches; they come in many guises, ostentatious paeans of praise in stone or extravagant words, or simple tablets of undoubted sincerity. There is a very different memorial in this little medieval church reflecting great thought, even if today it is only regarded as a curiosity. It is inscribed as being dedicated to the memory of Charles Smart Gaffin, for 25 years Vicar of Broadway, given by his wife and children for the free use of the parishioners of Broadway, Easter 1888. The memorial is entirely practical – it is a funeral bier: a heavy wheeled narrow vehicle, with a detachable stretcher and straps to hold the coffin in place, made with the negotiation of rough farm tracks in mind.

Just beyond the church take the path on the left signed to Broadway Tower, this is Coneygree Lane, and was once the Worcester/London road. Wrought iron gates (open) guard the way, suggesting the entry to a great estate. The map shows a mile long winding track to Middle Hill House on the wooded hillside. This was the home of a nineteenth century collector of unbridled enthusiasm and ambition. Manuscripts and books were his all consuming passion, so much so that he expressed the intention to assemble a personal library of every book, clearly a quite impossible goal.

The track, dampened by springs issuing out of the hillside and shaded by oak, chestnut, ash and sycamore is followed for just over half a mile. There are wild flowers in abundance, ramsons, campion, archangel, cow parsley, cranesbill, purple vetch, mouse-ear and those sticky things that we used to throw at people in our childhood — burdock. At a T-junction of paths, turn right, waymarked, soon to be out in the open and heading towards the woods at Knap Bank. You are now in the privately owned Broadway Country Park and to your left is an enclosure with deer. A magnificent beech, a giant among trees, marks the junction of paths at the edge of the wood. Here turn left. As a group of buildings is reached, the path joins a metalled estate road, again turn left with it. When the summit of the hill is almost reached look for the yellow waymark on the left. This is found on one of the enclosures. Pursue the waymarked route passing Rookery Barn, the refreshment centre of the park to your right and continuing with the path signed to Broadway Tower.

Broadway Tower

The sixty-five feet tall tower is often described as a folly and this is a pity for it tends to give the wrong impression. A folly has been defined as an expensive but useless structure usually associated with the eccentric rich. It has to be admitted that in a measure this is true of Broadway Tower, but what a marvellous contribution it has made to the landscape. Built in the grand manner, with rounded turrets, oriel windows and little balconies, it is altogether as handsome a fairy-tale folly as you could expect to find in the land. Clearly no expense was spared in its construction – indeed the sixth Earl of Coventry engaged the services of the leading architect of the day, James Wyatt. There must have been a great celebration on completion of the work in 1799.

It is said that the tower was built with the intention of using it as a signalling station to effect speedy communication between the Springhill Estate and the Earl's Worcester home, Croome Court. Its commanding position on the 1024 feet hill, would have had immense appeal to William Morris when he holidayed here with his friends Burne-Jones and Rossetti. A romantic place for romantically disposed people. The tower is open to visitors (see useful information section). In addition to enjoying the expansive view there is a William Morris exhibition, the Story of Sheep and Wool together with a History of the Tower.

At one time the tower was used by Sir Thomas Phillips in a logical extension of his book and manuscript interests, when he installed a printing press. Whatever the reasoning that prompted its building, there is no doubt that this is an excellent spot from which to play the age old game of picking out the distant high points. On a clear day, they say, you can see for ever, given similarly good conditions the Broadway canvas is reputed to take in twelve counties.

To complete the walk, turn left beyond the tower to descend the waymarked path back to Broadway which is reached in just over a mile of easy walking.

Walk 3: The Man who had Everything

Snowshill circuit

Route: Broadway — Broadway Coppice — Manor Farm — Shenberrow Hill (edge) — Snowshill — Great Brockhampton Farm — Manor Farm — Broadway

Map: 1:50,000 Landranger Sheet 150, 1:25,000 Pathfinder 1043 (SP03/13)

Distance: 9 miles

Parking: Leamington Road, Broadway

Toilets: Leamington Road, Broadway

The Walk

Turn left as you leave the Leamington Road car park and at the main street turn right to walk through the centre of the village with its busy shops and comfortably old buildings. At the green turn left along the Snowshill Road. The walk follows the Cotswold Way to the edge of Shenberrow Hill.

St. Michael's church is soon reached and although still youthful in relation to our ancient parish churches is worth a visit for its stained glass windows.

Saint Eadburgha is featured in the chancel, with the old Broadway church (visited in the last walk) in her hands. Eadburgha was a grand-daughter of King Alfred. Another royal saint is depicted in one of the chancel windows, Elizabeth of Hungary. This thirteenth century Hungarian princess was unfailing in her care for the poor. Her first husband, whom she had married at a very tender age, died during the crusades. Elizabeth eventually joined a religious order. The window illustrates the legend associated with her work which did not always find favour with others. Challenged on one of her charitable missions, delivering bread, she opened her basket to show roses not bread, a minor miracle which averted a wrathful response.

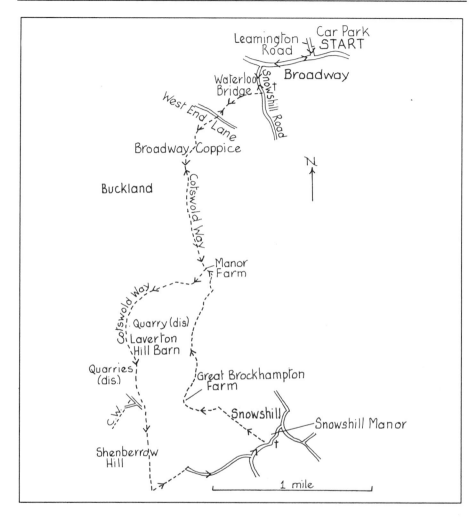

Another window has Broadway Tower as a background, it is always worthwhile taking a good look at backgrounds in stained glass for they often include local buildings or countryside. An example is the excellent window at Selbourne, in Hampshire. This was the famous naturalist, the Rev. Gilbert White's church, and his memorial window depicts St. Francis with over forty of the birds to be found in and around the village.

A little past the church take the path on the right signed to Buckland, Shenberrow and Cotswold Way. After a short distance cross a stile and follow the waymarked path over the fields. A plank bridge over a little stream is crossed, this is Waterloo Bridge, a far cry from the great stone bridge that spans the Thames. Continue on rising ground to meet and cross West End Lane. Here take the signed path climbing to Broadway Coppice. (Turn to take a backward look at the village spread out below.)

Take the path through the coppice which is soon left behind as the Cotswold Way is followed with trees on the left. When a wooden farm building by a tall ash tree is reached, turn right. Then almost immediately turn left to follow a broad track for just under half a mile to reach the buildings of Manor Farm.

Cross a stile and turn right signed to Shenberrow Hill and Stanton. There are views down to the little village of Buckland, reputed to have the oldest rectory in England.

The rising path deepens into a hollow way. Near the summit Laverton Hill Barn is passed on the left and Bredon Hill looms large on the landscape, remembered by the poet A.E.Housman with "In summertime on Bredon" from his famous collection "A Shropshire Lad."

Leave the Cotswold Way at the point where it makes a sharp right turn for Stanton. Continue forward and head for the double metal gates, slight right, and follow the blue arrowed bridleway for a little over half a mile with long-disused quarries on your right. Power lines follow part of the way and just before they run off to the right take the bridle path diagonally left over the fields.

Snowshill village soon comes into sight. Maintain your direction following the waymarked path. On reaching a metalled lane turn right (ignore the farm track on the left part way down the lane). At T-junction turn left to Snowshill to explore the village and perhaps visit Snowshill Manor. (Opening times in the Useful Information section.)

Set on a breezy hillside, Snowshill is the very essence of today's Cotswold village, mellowed stone and little gabled windows set in lichen-covered roofs. The larger houses with well-kept gardens running down to the road and smaller dwellings with doors opening on to the road make the most of their two feet or so of front garden. Generally, a symphony in stone and green untroubled by the clamour of heavy traffic.

Cottages at Snowshill

Snowshill Manor

That Snowshill Manor has a long history cannot be doubted, for there were people here long before the Domesday Book set out in 1086, in the interests of tax collection, to produce a comprehensive survey of the country. Over the centuries the house will have been home to many people: men, women and children, masters and servants, all enjoyed the shelter of its roof and the comfort of its fireside. It will have many stories to tell, one of a secret marriage that took place at midnight in 1604 for instance. Our concern is with one man, Charles Wade, for his story is surely the most interesting in all the five hundred years history of the present house.

Charles Wade was not a pale shadowy figure from a distant and half forgotten age, but a man of this century, although his interests were centred in the craftsmanship of the past. It is entirely appropriate that the fruits of his life-long collection should remain in this setting.

The house is full of surprises and at this point the narrative should end and leave the visitor to make his own discoveries. However, this book, like many another travel book, is likely to be read by armchair travellers, so even if all is not revealed at least a corner of the veil must be raised.

Charles was an enthusiastic collector, not of the cheque book flourishing bidder at fashionable auction houses variety, but a get out and about treasure hunter, ferreting out items of interest. While a great deal of his collection is valuable in itself, there are many once everyday items amongst the thousands of pieces on display.

He was not only a collector, but an architect, a craftsman and an excellent writer. His description of his travels whilst building up his collection, is a delightful essay which paints a vivid picture of his search. It is reproduced on one of the walls in the Manor and in a booklet published by the National Trust.

Charles started young, by the age of seven his pocket money was being carefully used to purchase items that took his fancy. Here perhaps were the formative days of his discretion. While his peers agonised over the rival merits of spending their precious weekly allowance on a ha'p'orth of toffees or a sherbet dip, Charles might have been exercising equal discernment over less transitory pleasures.

Despite this introduction, the visitor may soon begin to wonder if he is an intruder at the late home of a considerable eccentric. This view is almost certain to be formed, if after taking in the pleasures of the garden, the next port of call is the Priest's House.

Leaving the army at the conclusion of the first World War, Charles Wade discovered Snowshill Manor in a poor state of repair and bought it at once. His talents transformed the house and garden, reflecting the rescue of many Cotswold villages from dereliction, that has given them a new prosperity in this century. There are a series of gardens, each announced with a superscription, each a little sanctuary divided by walls and linked by stepped paths over the falling ground.

An old dovecote, a perquisite of the Lord of the Manor, provides a home for a dozen or so white doves. Unlike their ancestors, who were kept for both eggs and flesh, today's residents are more certain to survive the winter! Other outbuildings house a model village, a collection of hand-operated fire pumps and an assortment of farm implements.

The Priest's House has a handsome carving of St. George, dragon at his feet, about to strike the hour, the voice of the clock that is within the house itself. It is at the Priest's House that the unsuspecting visitor is suddenly taken by the throat and rendered breathless with astonishment. For beyond its leaded lights are sights unparalleled in any other National Trust property.

The Priest's House was where Charles Wade lived, the Manor House being devoted to the exhibition of his increasing collection of craftsmanship. Indeed this was his stated intention, the collection of craftsmanship, and it is displayed in many forms. The kitchen is seen first, you cannot enter but must be an onlooker. Entry would be almost impossible without creating an avalanche of the myriad items that are present on every surface, from floor to ceiling and wall to wall. It is reported that the Priests House has been retained virtually as Wade left it. It takes a big leap of the imagination to see anybody living in this environment.

A chair, very much like a child's swing is suspended from the ceiling and positioned at the head of the table. A large hall porter's chair is by the hearth. Thereafter the eye and mind have to focus very hard to take in the contents of the room. It is not so much what is there but the quantity. There is a lost property office-sized clutch of umbrellas, enough spits to meet the needs of a medieval banqueting hall, complemented by a host of wooden spoons. There are knives and bottles, clogs and little barrels, items of horse harness, parts of an old clock and that essential requirement of every well-equipped kitchen, an anti-poacher gun. It's the advanced version of Kims Game for the memory man's championship of the world.

All this is set at naught compared with the bedroom. I must call it that, since that is where he slept. But it is quite a while before the bed is actually spotted, boxed into a corner with hanging curtains and a little ladder to climb. The rest of this very large room is an extraordinary mix contriving to give the impression of the props department of a film studio with a long string of bizarre movies behind it.

A raised gallery suggests the executive class accommodation of a ship in the days of sail, an impression confirmed by a model of just such a ship. Lamps hang from the ceiling, while the walls are covered with funeral hatchments, shields, helmets and body armour. The furniture includes a sedan chair, old chests, a large globe and a candle-lit altar. We therefore have, at least in part, the setting for an olden day and probably not legal, adventure of the sea. A days of old when knights were bold epic, a drama with strong religious undertones and to round it up a very large leather bound tome suggests Merlin's book of magic spells.

If the reader thinks this all a bit over the top, suspend judgment until you see for yourself, as the estate agents are apt to say – this property must be viewed.

The Manor House creates quite a different feeling of harmony and confirms Charles Wade as the supreme collector, even to the most cursory of viewers. The rooms are all named, reflecting their position in the house or their contents. A score or more Samurai warriors leap out at any who dare intrude into the Green Room, lacquered Chinese cabinets and porcelain take up the eastern theme elsewhere.

There are arms and armour, heraldic devices, drums from Waterloo, truncheons, sticks and staves. The commonplace of yesteryear is found in a hundred different artifacts, the tools of the carpenter and cobbler, lacemaker, spinner, weaver and many more. There is both mousetrap and medicine chest, the magic and the mundane.

In The Room of a Hundred Wheels, models of farm carts from many counties, early bicycles, coaches and a variety of perambulators from three centuries all compete for attention. There's more, much more, but Seventh Heaven, a collection of childhood toys, is something to which all can relate.

Charles Wade made his gift to the nation for all to enjoy. The pleasure of a visit could only be improved if the man himself were there to personally conduct his guests around his house of treasures . . . but perhaps he does in spirit.

Return to Broadway

After visiting Snowshill Manor, retrace your steps through the village to take the path on the right just beyond Oat House. The path descends to the valley towards a pond, equipped with barrels for nesting wild fowl. At the foot of the valley leave the broad track, as signed, and follow the waymarked path with hedge/fence on your left. Changes of direction are all waymarked, continue forward when Great Brockhampton Farm comes into view on the hillside ahead to meet a metalled farm lane. Here turn left for a few yards then fish-hook right on a broad track.

Many incidental interests are met when walking, weather vanes are one and the farm boasts a mounted huntsman, a not uncommon subject. The wide track is followed for nearly a mile to Manor Farm.

The landscape is a broad canvas by a master painter, across the valley Snowshill is seen to perfection, the lush green countryside a perfect foil to its old stone. Bridleways and paths wind over the hillside, inviting further exploration, whilst the woods and coppices fit the contours of the hills in contrast to the insensitive plantings sometimes met elsewhere.

When Manor Farm is reached, rejoin the Cotswold Way and return by your outward route with good views of Broadway.

Walk 4: Shuffleboard

Stanton – Stanway – Shenberrow Hill

Route: Stanton – Stanway – Lidcombe Wood – Shenberrow Hill – Stanton

Map: 1:50,000 Landranger 150, 1:25,000 Pathfinder 1043 (SP03/13)

Distance: 6 miles

Parking: By Stanton village club

Stanton and Stanway are twin villages lying back from the B4632 and linked by the umbilical cords of a country road and a field path.

Stanton

Stanton is another splendid Cotswold village, each one seems better than the last, and some, with justification, have claimed it as one of the best. In common with other Cotswold villages it has benefited from careful restoration work, in this instance at the hands of Sir Philip Stott whose home it was for some thirty years from 1906.

The village is immaculate, looking its best in the kindly but searching light of May. The stone enhanced by roses and clematis on the walls, with skilful conversion of barns and a dairy to residential use. It receives its share of tourists but it is a peaceful invasion not fuelled by commercial attractions and the Americans renting the holiday cottages must feel they are truly vacationing in a piece of old England. This is a perfect place from which to start a country walk, with a visit to the church as a curtain raiser or finale to the day's excursion.

Architecturally the church of St. Michael and All Angels claims Norman birth, with its earliest Rector recorded in 1269 as John de Tueing but it is believed a Saxon church would have existed here. Early in the ninth century, Kenulph, King of Mercia, gave the living of Stanton to the abbey at Winchcombe which he founded. The

Church of St. Michael and All Angels, Stanton

abbey housed the shrine of his son Kenelm, saint and martyr, the circumstance of his death and the legends will be explored in a later chapter.

Today St. Michael's reflects the image held in the minds of many people of the village church. The yellow blossom of a large laburnum tree waves visitors into the neatly kept churchyard with its tombs of past worshippers. Within, the church is cool and dark with past and present linked in many ways. Fragments of old glass, secretly collected in pots from Hailes Abbey at the dissolution, are found in the east window. Two pulpits, one of the fourteenth century and a later, canopied pulpit from which the great Charles Wesley once preached.

Once when I was in the church, a tiny mouse ran down the chancel and did a circuit of the old pulpit. What nourishment could there possibly be here, not yet harvest festival, surely there was a better living to be found elsewhere? No wonder the phrase as poor as a church mouse was once common currency. The incident a reminder of John Betjeman's brilliant poem "Diary of a Church Mouse."

At the back of the church three pews, seats of farmers and shepherds whose dogs accompanied them everywhere, bear the marks of chains. A relic of the past and a reminder of the great heritage of sheep farming in the Cotswolds. At one time Tewkesbury Abbey had an enormous flock of sheep upon the hills around Stanton.

There is a box, perhaps a document chest, dated 1704, bearing the name Elizabeth Farley. The visitor may be left wondering who was Elizabeth Farley, what did she keep in her long chest and why is it now in the church?

Some of the memorials of the 18th and 19th centuries take a little patience to read and one wonders whether people were better valued in that day or their virtues simply overstated. When Frances, the third daughter of Reginald and Frances Wynniatt died in 1808 at the early age of 19 her parents were grief-stricken. The memorial they erected in the church reflects this and paints a picture of what we might regard today as an unnatural goodness in one so young.

It reads:

"Cut off in the morning of her life her many amiable virtues had endeared her to all who knew her. Sensible and prudent in all her actions she lived unspotted from the world and untainted with any of its vanities. The qualities of her heart and understanding were alike happy and full of promise. The latter she had improved by diligent cultivation and the first she exercised by yielding implicitly whenever an occasion presented itself, to the benevolent sympathies of her nature. Her manners were most engaging and bespoke a sweetness of disposition ever studious to contribute to the happiness of those around her. The natural sensibility of her heart was still further refined and exalted by a genuine sense of religion and unfeigned piety, wholly unaffected and unostentatious but visible in its constant influence upon the tenor of her thoughts and actions. Upheld by the animating prospect of a future and better start of existence, she supported the lingering illness which brought her to a premature grave with exemplary patience and cheerful resignation.

Her afflicted parents have erected this marble, unwilling that so much unassuming merit should descend to the grave unnoticed and pass away unrecorded."

What a poignant picture it paints!

The Walk

Leave the car park and turn right. Opposite is Stanton Court, with the upper storey visible over the clipped yew hedge. After a short distance turn right again, signed to Stanway and take the road through the village for 250 yards. At a bend in the road take the path on the left signed Cotswold Way, Stanway 2Km. Soon turn right and follow the waymarked path across the fields.

To the right is seen the viaduct of the former Gloucestershire and Warwickshire Railway, now enthusiastically run by a railway society with ambitious plans for expansion. The field path leads on to Stanway Park with its mature trees. There is a fine avenue of chestnuts, a beautiful copper beech, great oaks and that most splendid of all parkland trees, the Cedar of Lebanon.

It is a tree that gets several mentions in the bible, Psalm 92 ". . . The righteous shall flourish like the palm tree: he shall grow like a cedar in Lebanon," and in the Book of Kings there are many references to the use of cedar in the building of Solomon's Temple. No wonder it is to be found in many churchyards, sometimes overtopping the tower, as well as in the gardens of the great country houses.

About a mile from Stanton, the path reaches the road, here turn left. Just opposite is the cricket pitch and the suitably rural thatched pavilion. Follow the road bending to the left to pass the church and the gate-house of Stanway House.

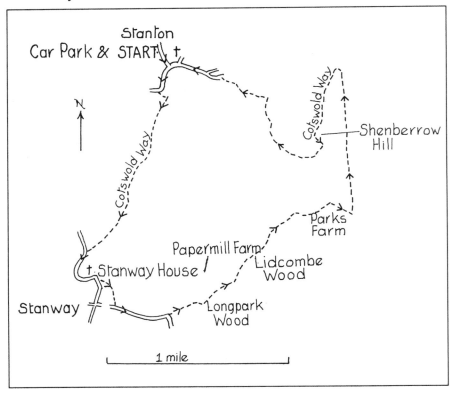

Stanway House

Stanway House, a Jacobean Manor House, belongs to the Earl of Wemyss. It is only in recent years that it has been open to visitors and is well worth the effort of returning on another occasion if it is not possible to visit during the course of this walk.

The Tithe Barn should not be missed when visiting the house for it represents a thousand years of what might be called taxation history. It has great thick walls of stone, a beautifully beamed roof of oak which has stood here for some six hundred and fifty years.

The nice thing about a visit to Stanway is that it has that lived in feeling. Family photographs on mantlepieces, books stacked on a table and a little pile of sheet music leave the impression that as soon as the last visitor of the afternoon has left the family will reclaim its own.

Some snippets from the house and its history may serve to whet the appetite for a personal visit. The Audit Room carries on a long tradition, here tenants come to pay their quarterly rent. To facilitate payment rent tables were a feature of the great estates and in most places these only remain as a curiosity. The revolving tables had drawers in which the tenants' rent books were kept, with locked compartments to accommodate the payment.

The Great Hall is impressive, the walls hung with tapestries and funeral hatchments and a magnificent mullioned bay window looking out to the church. It is not difficult to see this as the setting for the Manorial Court, the last being held here in 1800. The Hall is a place of contrasts, the administration of local justice set against the fun and games of family gatherings as evidenced in the remarkable table set along one wall. Not a banqueting table as you might suppose at first glance but a Shuffleboard Table. It is a large piece of equipment for a game that was the forerunner of shove ha'penny. It was constructed from a single oak planted on the estate in 1300 and felled to make the twenty three feet long table three hundred years later. Highest possible score is 20 but in nearly four hundred years of play the record is 15 and this has only been achieved four times.

Four postage stamps stuck to the high ceiling are pointed out to visitors as evidence of a less formal game. A coin with a stamp stuck to it was spun with the intention of getting the stamp to stick to the ceiling. James Barrie was a visitor to Stanway and it is no surprise that this game appealed to the author of Peter Pan, the story of the boy that didn't grow up.

There are day beds in the parlour, a hint of luxury that many would envy. Here the Lords of the Manor laid in state before their funeral. The last to enjoy the dignity of this rite was Old Smelly, a favourite dog, we shall pay our own respects to him a little later.

The two genealogical tables on view at Stanway will be a matter of envy to amateur researchers into their own antecedents. The first table of the Wemyss family starts in 1202. It's a little breath-taking when you pause to think about it and set it in the context of history. King John, "Johnny Lackland," was on the throne, Magna Carta still thirteen years in the future.

Even more impressive is the table that charts the descent of the Tracey family taking us back to King Egbert and the year 836. If you have the time and patience to scan through this table and its footnotes, much will be revealed. Taken at random, here are some newsworthy items. William de Tracey was one of the four knights, who taking Henry II at his word, murdered Beckett in his cathedral at Canterbury.

When Sir William Tracey died in 1530 his corpse was burnt as that of a heretic due to the controversial nature of his will. On a more pleasing note, Henrietta, a Maid of Honour to Queen Charlotte, married Viscount Hereford, and was responsible for the tree plant-ings on the hills above the village in 1800. Like Wren and St. Paul's Cathedral . . . if you seek her memorial look around.

There is a portrait of Francis Charteris, the 10th Earl of Wemyss. He holds a considerable record having sat in Parliament for 75 years, starting his long career in 1841.

The grounds should not be neglected, for if the ghosts of the past walk, then surely they walk here, and not only human ghosts. Behind the house the land rises steeply, crossing the former lake, to reach the pyramid erected in 1750 to honour John Tracey who had died 15 years earlier. It is from this elevated position that one gets the perfect view of the house in its setting of mature parkland trees, the church hard by and the timeless hills beyond. Behind the pyramid there are the remains of the pond dug to feed the cascade that tumbled down the hillside from the pyramid to add its waters to the lake. It must have been a delightful prospect in its day.

From the pyramid descend towards the house but when the terrace that was once the lake is reached turn left to the dogs' graveyard, which is found within a small hedge enclosure. Here the family dogs have been buried; Darling Dandy 1930-1944; Faithful Stella 1883-1898 and the headstone to Old Smelly who had lain in state in the parlour. The Latin inscription is headed by crossed bones and honoured by what I suppose the Herald's office would call dogs rampant.

The inscription reads:

Memoriae Fraganti
Old Smelly
OBIT MCMLXXX aetatis XVI
canis
sanguine quamvis ferocifacile redolentis
suavitate ramen sua quam stirpe redolentions
hoc qualecunque momumentum
IACOBVS NEIDPATH dominus
proneprisque LITTLE SMELLY
sculptoruqe RORY YOVNG
pietaris ergo erigendum curaverunt
anno salutis canum
MXMLXXXIV

By the garden wall there are two oval squint holes, a small challenge to the photographer to capture the church within their framing, a pleasant memento of a visit to this delightful place

The Walk, continued

A little beyond the gate-house of Stanway House the path takes a left turn by the estate yard and an old yew with a surrounding seat. The pink herb robert, a member of the geranium family, grows on the wall. It contrives to flower for a long period from April onwards producing three different colours in its leaves.

After passing through the remains of an old orchard, meet the road, turn left and bid a temporary farewell to the Cotswold Way. Follow the road for about 600 yards and where it bends to the right, go forward towards cottages, taking the left of two bridleways, which edges Longpark Wood. It is a cool shady way and has the appearance of a hollow way of some age. Below to the left will be seen Papermill Farm alongside the stream, damned long ago to provide a head of water to power the mill, a facility now enjoyed by a little flock of ducks.

The bridleway is waymarked, at a large beech tree, about level with Papermill Farm, bear left with the track. When the path divides by a stone building take the centre path running roughly north-east. By now you may be hearing some strange sounds, like some pre-historic monster working itself up to do battle, it is in fact a hydraulic ram pumping water.

The path winds upwards through Lidcomb Wood, with ramsons in profusion, its pungent smell will announce its presence, old socks or garlic according to the delicacy of your thinking. Its white starred flowers compensate handsomely for its less than attractive perfume.

In just under a mile from the point where you left the road, emerge into the open to meet a wide track. Go forward on this with woods to your left. When the trees fall back, ignore turnings to left and right and continue in the direction of Snowshill for about 300 yards. As the track swings to the right take the waymarked bridleway on the left which runs north. This is followed with a stone wall on your left for a little over half a mile, passing through several metal gateways en route.

When a junction is reached with a metalled road, turn left and in a few yards join the Cotswold Way on the left. This waymarked path is now followed all the way back to Stanton. The path passes over Shenberrow Hill with the remains of an iron age hill fort at its edge.

After passing through a gate by Shenberrow buildings watch for the Cotswold Way waymark and follow the path which drops steeply through a cleft in the hills. The edge of Stanton is reached after about three-quarters of a mile. Shortly after passing the old preaching cross, turn right to regain your starting point at the village club car park.

Walk 5: Days of Storm

Hailes Abbey

Route: Stanway — Wood Stanway — Stumps Cross — Beckbury — Hailes Abbey — Didbrook — Stanway

Map: 1:50,000 Landranger Sheet 150, Pathfinder 1043 (SO 03/13) and 1067 (SP 02/12)

Distance: 6 miles

Parking: Informal off road possible at Stanway, near Memorial Hall on Wood Stanway road

---

The walk starts from the small crossroad formed by the B4077 at its junction with the Stanway/Wood Stanway road. Here, set up where all can see, and sometimes remember, is the memorial to the Men of Stanway 1914-1918. It depicts St. George slaying the dragon, the inscription, now fading, reads:

> For A Tomb
> They Have An Altar
> For Lamentation
> Memory
> For Pity
> Prayer

The Walk

From the memorial take the Stow road, passing the village Post Office and the Old Bake House. We are in a well-wooded countryside and the ridge seen ahead and half right has a fine line of trees on the skyline which immediately attracts the eye.

About 300 yards from the crossroads join the Cotswold Way, signed off on the right to Wood Stanway. At first this is a narrow path between hedges, much overgrown in summer and a sure recipe for wet legs on a dewy morning or after rain. The way is defended by a series of natural obstacles: barbed wire brambles, anti-personnel nettles, menacing hog-weed, man traps of trailing roots and similar delights designed to keep the walker concentrating on his feet rather than the view.

Having escaped from the imprisoning walls of the hedgerow, take the waymarked path over the fields to Wood Stanway which is reached in about half a mile. Wood Stanway is a tiny hamlet, a few cottages sandwiched between two farms on the lane that is its link with the outside world.

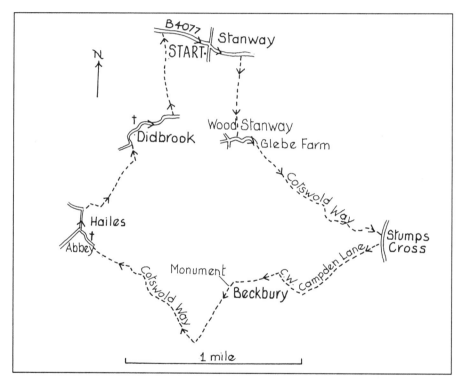

On reaching the lane, turn left. By Glebe Farm the road narrows to become a track. Continue forward signed to Stumps Cross and Temple Guiting, heading towards the tree-topped ridge. After the farm, pass through a metal gate and take the path uphill, shortly bearing to the left as signed. Cross the stile by a metal gate and bear half right uphill. Go towards the power lines but watch for the arrow marked posts that signal a change of direction slightly left, directing you towards the ridge.

The view opens out as height is gained with the long line of the Malverns, Bredon Hill and Dumbleton Hill. Below, the gable ends and roof tops of Wood Stanway peep out above the trees.

Beyond a gate/stile, head towards a group of farm buildings, as these are neared, pass through a five-barred gate and swing right as way-marked. (A footpath diversion made some years ago.) On reaching a further metal gate and stile, turn left as directed by a waymark. Soon a steep ladder stile (by power lines) lifts you over a dry stone wall. This is followed on your left until a waymark post directs you up a slope towards a clump of trees.

You have been climbing steadily since leaving Wood Stanway and have reached the line of trees that were the object of admiration at the start of the walk. A suitable moment to pause for a breather and enjoy the expansive view with the distant hills, farms dotted here and there within the pattern of pasture, plough and forest. Not sombre conifers, but glorious mixed woodland with its many shades of green richly clothing the hills, riding comfortably the contours of the land. An ordinary but extraordinary landscape, one that might well be envied by those from more distant, more dramatic climes or from the nearer flat lands and often treeless landscape of our own fen country.

Turn left with the path to reach the road at Stumps Cross. With what appears to be the origin of its name at your feet as the wall is crossed at the road edge. Set in the wall is a post box of Edward VII vintage. Turn right along the road for a short distance to join the bridleway on the right signed to Farmcote, Hailes Abbey and Winchcombe. This is Campden Lane, an old Cotswold track, broad at this point and lined with mature trees, beech, lime, ash and a single larch.

After passing some partly ruined farm buildings, continue forward beyond a metal gate until a clump of trees is reached in about 300 yards, here turn right. Since Stumps Cross, you have been on the summit tableland with the views restricted. Now they begin to open up again with the radio masts, six miles distant as the crow flies, marking the southern end of Cleeve Common.

About a quarter of a mile after leaving Campden Lane the path turns left to follow a dry stone wall beyond which a bank falls steeply away with oak, ash and beech clinging to the slope. Soon the hilltop camp at Beckbury is reached, protected on the less steep sides by bank and ditch.

Beckbury is a natural defensive site where the occupants could watch an enemy struggle up the northern or western side of the hill, and await the moment to launch their counter attack upon a breathless invader. At the western edge of the camp is a clump of beech trees and a monument said to be the spot where Cromwell watched the destruction of Hailes Abbey.

Thomas Cromwell was Henry VIII's chief minister for seven years during the dramatic period of the dissolution of the monasteries. He had spent much time abroad, both as a soldier and businessman. Cromwell became a lawyer and later entered Parliament, growing rapidly in power and influence. By 1533 he was Chancellor of the Exchequer and two years later Vicar General, playing a major part in the Dissolution. His was a story of an incredible success and yet it was a rise that was to end in death and disgrace. In the spring of 1540 he was made Earl of Essex, then Lord Great Chamberlain, but within the space of less than two months he had been charged with both heresy and treason with the inevitable consequence. Perhaps Cromwell's biggest crime in the king's eyes was his part in selecting Anne of Cleeves as Henrys fourth bride.

From Beckbury pass through the clump of beeches and then swing left to follow the waymarked falling path through the fields to meet a broad track in about half a mile. Here turn right, still on the Cotswold Way, and descend, with Hailes Wood on the right, to reach Hailes Abbey after three-quarters of a mile

Hailes Abbey

Hailes Abbey was conceived in a storm, born late in the monastic building boom and perished in the tidal wave that engulfed the already declining religious foundations three hundred years later.

The establishment of monastic houses seems to have been something of a growth industry in the 12th century and in medieval times they may have been counted in four figures. Hailes had its beginnings in a storm at sea. Richard, Earl of Cornwall, second son of King John, felt his life in danger during the autumn gales of October 1242. A storm at sea is frightening enough in these days. To have been in the midst of a howling gale on the frailer vessels of the time would have been a daunting experience for the bravest of men. There comes a moment when there is only one thing left to do – pray. And pray Richard did, vowing that if only he could be saved he would found a monastery.

It is not unknown for promises made in such circumstances to be forgotten when the danger has passed, but Richard did not forget. Four years later, thirty men, a mix of monks and lay brothers arrived from Hampshire to signal the foundation of Hailes Abbey. It was beautifully situated in a sheltered position beneath the hill, close by the little church that still serves the community. Springs in the hillside provided a good supply of

Hailes Abbey

clean water for washing and to maintain the fish ponds. Clearly there was much to be done, with a church and all the ancillary accommodation to be constructed from scratch on what we would today call a green field site.

In November 1251 there was great rejoicing at Hailes to mark the dedication of the Abbey with an exalted company assembled for the ceremony. The great and powerful of the land were led by Richard's brother, Henry II with his wife, Eleanor of Provence. Accompanying them were members of the court, bishops from near and far and all the local gentry of sufficient importance to be invited.

Hailes needed money to survive. It is all very well to build but day to day expenses go on for ever. The monks had to be fed, the buildings maintained, the poor, the sick and the old to be cared for and many other commitments. The foundation was aided by its farming activities, sheep the great providers, by rents from lands settled upon them and from the incomes of manors and churches. But at times they were struggling (literally) to keep a roof over their heads.

Pilgrimages to shrines of the saints or to venerate holy relics were more common in medieval England than they are today. They often represented a good source of income to those institutions fortunate enough to have a suitable object of devotion. Or sufficiently astute to acquire one. The shrine of Thomas a Becket at Canterbury, for example, was a place of pilgrimage soon after his murder in 1170 until its destruction nearly 400 years later. As a new foundation, Hailes did not give shelter to the bones of a saint like nearby Winchcombe with its shrine to the young Kenelm or a prized item such as a splinter of wood reputed to be from the true cross.

In 1270, Edmund, son of the founder, remedied the defect in the Abbey's inventory. He obtained for them a phial said to contain the Blood of Christ, an awesome relic if genuine and certain to attract a large number of pilgrims to Hailes. Given the circumstances of the crucifixion and resurrection it required a great deal of faith to accept that it was ever collected in the first place or survived for 1200 years in the second. Or that any right thinking person would part with it for mere money. Its authenticity was said to have been vouched for by no less a person than the Patriarch of Jerusalem, who was subsequently elected Pope.

Who could tell whether the Patriarch was convinced of the genuine nature of the phial to which he gave his authoritative testimony? Did Edmund fully believe he carried to Hailes the most precious relic of Christianity? Did the Abbot, surely not a simple man, believe he was receiving into his charge the blood of God made man? Who could say? Who dare say? Even for that matter, dare think? Perhaps the expression of disbelief required more courage than a profession of faith. The pilgrims believed and came year by year, down the centuries until the Commissioners appointed under Thomas Cromwell, with the authority of Henry VIII, came to Hailes in the autumn of 1538. The holy relic, the object of veneration for 268 years, was seized and taken to London for analysis: an infamous, unthinkable blasphemy, or the revelation of a fraud upon thousands of the faithful? We need not believe that the Commissioners actions were totally motivated by the desire to protect the humble pilgrim. Indeed if they believed they bowed the knee to the Holy Blood, their act of piety and worship was not lessened by a possible deception imposed upon them by the unscrupulous.

The sequel to the Commissioners' visit to Hailes came swiftly and . . . after much boulting and sifting a report was made to Cromwell. Whatever the facilities that were available for making a proper analysis, the relic was declared a fake, simply a compound of honey and a colouring agent. As others may have been tempted to say at the time, but would have been wise not to, "They would say that wouldn't they."

The leaves of autumn of the following year had hardly settled on the Abbey gardens before the chill wind of winter brought the end. On Christmas Eve 1539, the Abbot and his monks bowed to the inevitable and surrendered the Abbey to Henry's representatives.

What of Hailes today? In course of time it passed into the hands of the National Trust with the day to day running managed by English Heritage.

For the most part there are only the stumps of walls to be seen. Today's pilgrim may stand by the spot behind the high altar where the shrine protecting the holy relic once stood. The cloister arches and walls remain in part to aid the imagination to overcome the ravages of its destruction. The site exudes a strong sense of peace, the atmosphere of tranquillity enhanced by the backdrop of tall chestnut trees, their candles strangely symbolic of the days that were.

From the Abbey turn left, leaving the Cotswold Way (which continues to Winchcombe) and follow the road for 300 yards. Bend right with the road and after 200 yards or so take the path on the right signed to Stanway and follow this over the fields. On reaching the road at Didbrook turn right and walk towards the village. At a junction take the road signed to Wood Stanway soon to reach the church.

St. George's Church, Didbrook.

Legend has it that the bullet pock-marked door of the church has its origin in the Lancastrian defeat at nearby Tewkesbury in 1471. Bloody Meadow near the River Severn, graphically recalls the loss of life, more died as they tried to reach the safety of the opposite bank, others unsuccessfully sought sanctuary in the Benedictine Abbey. Some fled further afield taking refuge in the church at Didbrook but to no avail, nemesis overtook them and they were put to death. The origins of the bullet holes have been called into question. Alternative explanations include a possible skirmish in the conflict of the 1640s or target practice by the irreligious of a later century.

The church seems warm and welcoming, an atmosphere encouraged in the west window, dedicated "To the memory of all Pilgrims who have worshipped here"; in stained glass are scenes from the life of the village and church: baptisms and confirmation, marriage, death, children in school and at play.

In the neatly kept churchyard is a seat given in memory of a local

VC, William Holmes of the Grenadier Guards, who failed to survive the Great War by just one month.

From the church turn left up the road and in about 300 yards take the path on the left which is followed for half a mile to reach the road near Stanway. Here turn right and in a quarter of a mile meet the crossroads where St. George still stands guard..

Walk 6:
Leafy Lanes and Tangled Tracks

Sudeley Castle

Route: Hailes – Farmcote – Lynes Barn – Campden Lane – Deadmanbury Gate – Campden Lane – Roel Gate – Spoonley Wood – Home Parks – Winchcombe – Puck Pit Lane – Hailes

Map: 1:50,000 Landranger Sheet 163 and bottom edge of Sheet 150, 1:25,000 Pathfinder 1043 (SP 03/13) very small section (can be dispensed with if you don't already own it), Pathfinder 1067 (SO 02/12)

Distance: 10 miles

Parking: At Hailes for visitors to the Abbey

Caution: Part of the route, a section of Campden Lane, may be overgrown but not impassable, those wearing shorts may expect to be scratched or stung and probably both.

The walk starts from Hailes and if you have not yet seen the Abbey, see last chapter, now may be your chance. Hailes church should also be visited. It was not mentioned in the last chapter in order to avoid it being overshadowed by the more dramatic aspects of the Abbey.

Hailes Church

The church sparkles in the sunlight, an invitation to spend a few minutes within its walls. Restoration work in 1905 and important work in 1960-70 has left it in very good order. It is full of interest and the visitor will appreciate it the more if he has time to walk round with the excellent guide written by Lord Sudeley.

The church is at least a hundred years older than the Abbey. Although its exact age seems to be in doubt, it must be well on its way to celebrating its nine hundredth birthday. The one time glory of its neighbour, the Abbey, is recalled in at least two ways. First the old tiles set in the floor by the altar and above by glass, removed from the Abbey to Toddington church and at the 1905 restoration by Hugh Andrews transferred back to Hailes. The tiles have a story to tell in themselves and should be viewed guide book in hand.

It will be the wall paintings that are likely to take most people's attention. They could well have been lost but for the energetic fund raising and careful work completed in 1972. It is St. Christopher who greets the visitor, a giant of a man. In legend he carried Christ as a child over a turbulent river, symbolic of course, since he is believed to have lived around 250AD.

Hailes Church

On the south wall is a hunting scene, while to the left of the altar is another familiar saint, Catherine. The legends that surround St. Catherine are fanciful in the extreme, but the message they convey is one of steadfastness to her faith. The Hailes' painting depicts her as a woman of learning but she is often shown with the spiked wheel on which she was impaled. Hence the Catherine Wheel of our firework celebrations: it would be a nice touch if her feast day was the 5th of November but is inconveniently later in that month.

There are a number of other paintings and emblems which are fully described in the guide. It is believed that these date from the Abbey's early days. They are beautifully executed with a draughtsman-like expertise and it is tempting to speculate on their creators. Could it be that a monkish scribe, accustomed to the delicate work of book illumination, was the hand that so carefully decorated the walls of this little church? The liberation from the close confines of the parchment page to the broad canvas of the church walls reflected in the sweeping lines of the larger dimension.

The Walk

Leave Hailes on the Cotswold Way, signed to Farmcote, and make your way uphill with Hailes Wood on the left and orchards on the right. There is coppiced hazel on both sides of the track, a most useful tree for the countryman, making thatch pegs, hurdle fencing, bean sticks and wands for the water diviner.

Once clear of the wooded edges, the Cotswold Way leaves the track to make for Beckbury. However, our route continues forward to meet the narrow lane taking us to Farmcote, with its manor house and ancient church, in their hill top isolation.

It is a tiny place, so small that one wonders if the camp at Beckbury was home to more families than ever Farmcote nurtured. The church, St. Faith's, now towerless, almost takes on the appearance of a barn, except for its neat windows and very good order . . . the granary of God the poet might say. The aisle floor is almost taken up with two memorial stones covering the vaults of the Baker family, including Arabella, who died in June 1765 only 17 weeks old. The altar is a wooden table carrying a slab of stone, a pre-Reformation tradition. Many of these stone altars were swept away, statues were toppled and images vanquished, just as the wall paintings at Hailes, and in many another church,

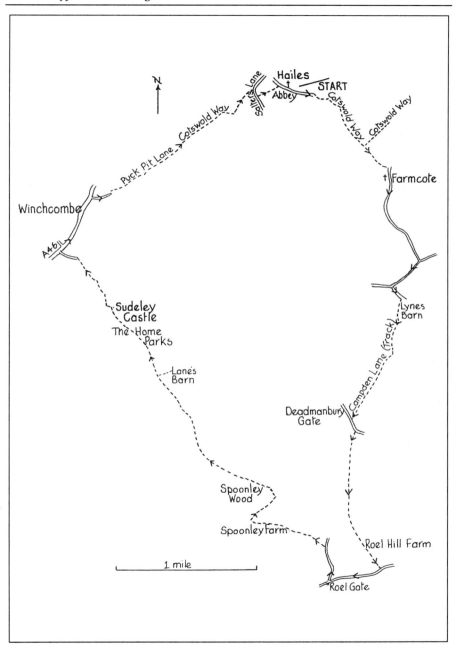

disappeared under the whitewash brush. To the left of the altar two long dead parishioners lie in the last elegant repose. The name of Stratford appears on a memorial. We shall meet a member of this family in a slightly surprising connection when we walk into Winchcombe.

On leaving the church continue along the lane, edged here and there with mallow and poppy, for three-quarters of a mile. At a junction take the right turn, signed to Winchcombe, and follow it for a quarter of a mile. Here the chalk loving scabious is one of the wild flowers that has found a haven on the banks by the hedgerows.

Take the lane on the left (signed unfit for motor vehicles) and after passing Lynes Barn join Campden Lane on the right. It rises steadily and after a while disappears into a deep and overgrown hollow way. The depth of the path beneath the surrounding cultivated land advertises the great age of the track. The minor agony of nettles and brambles does not last for ever. The summit is reached by the abandoned but accurately named Hill Top Cottage, with only a clump of lupins in the now neglected garden to give a splash of colour. Perhaps the cottage will yet be saved.

The path continues, again overgrown, but the more boots that pass this way the less danger there is of the path disappearing. On escaping to the road at Deadmanbury Gate, turn left along the quiet lane. The name Deadmanbury Gate is intriguing and a possible connection might be assumed with the nearby Long Barrow Bank.

In about 200 yards, as the lane bends to the left, take the path on the right (note this is forward right and going south). Still Campden Lane, but far more comfortable walking, this is followed for just over a mile. Soon after passing Roel Hill Farm a lane is reached, turn right and meet Roel Gate crossroads in about 700 yards. Here turn right, along the Salt Way from Hailes.

The Salt Ways are very old roads, dating back to at least Saxon times, the pack horse routes taken by the traders distributing that essential food additive, not just for flavouring but for preservation. This road is one of a network of tracks spreading out from the Worcestershire salt producing town of Droitwich.

After a quarter of a mile take the lane on the left which runs down to Spoonley Farm. The banks at the side have common spotted orchid, scabious and the elder flower, another harvest from the hedgerow for the home wine maker. The descending lane offers good views with Winchcombe tucked comfortably under the hills. About 400 yards after passing Spoonley Farm take the path on the right found by a small group of mature ash trees. (Note: an alternative path back to Winchcombe from Spoonley Farm is to follow the waymarked Windrush Way via Waterhatch, No Mans Patch and the Home Parks. The waymarking is a halved circle part white, part black). Follow the path for about a quarter of a mile until a narrow gap is reached between two woods. Take the path on the left through Spoonley Wood to emerge on its north west edge. The wood is damp and has encouraged the growth of thistles, some reaching a height of eight feet.

Beyond the wood turn left onto the path along its edge and pursue this to the bottom of the field. As a broad track is seen ahead, turn right on an indistinct path which crosses the bottom of the field. After a short distance pass through the hedge and take the waymarked path over the field with further waymarking on a power line post. Cross the fence through a small patch of conifers and over a further field, with farm buildings seen in the distance directly ahead. Before the far boundary of the field is reached the path swings to the left. It then becomes a broad track which continues after crossing a small stream almost lost in the thick growth on its banks. Remain with the track, passing a reservoir on your left. When the track swings to the right, to Lanes Barn, leave it and take the path over the stile on the left as directed by sign and continue forward as arrowed. Sudeley Castle comes into view. Cross a further stile and follow the field edge with hedge on the right. At the end of the field bear left for a few paces, then cross a stile entering the Home Parks of Sudeley Castle. Follow the path diagonally left across the field. The stile on the other side is seen to the left of a large tree. The path meets the south west corner of the Castle gardens. After passing through a kissing gate take the path along the line of the fence. Then follow the waymarked path that runs north-westerly through the grounds to meet the road by the Sudeley Castle holiday cottages.

Sudeley Castle

"Winds of change" might have been coined expressly to describe the long history of Sudeley Castle. Winds that were set fair for its fortune, sudden gales whose wrath played havoc with its roofs and left it an abandoned wreck and gentler refreshing winds that led to its partial restoration.

The castle is set a little above Winchcombe on the lower slopes of Sudeley Hill, on a site favoured since pre-Norman times. Much of today's Sudeley has its origins at the hand of Ralph Boteler, after successfully serving two kings in the long running wars with the French, he was created Baron Sudeley in 1441. He built a castle that was a home and a home that was a castle alongside St. Mary's Church.

Boteler was on the losing side in the dispute between the houses of Lancaster and York, with Edward IV taking the throne in 1461. Subsequently Boteler found it expedient to part with Sudeley to the King, setting in motion a long history of changes of ownership.

Conflict again took a part. In the Civil War the house was held first for the King, but succumbed to the Parliamentarians early in 1643. Its new and temporary garrison indulged in the excesses of plunder and pillage that is so often a feature of wars however just in spirit. The castle reverted to the Royalists but surrendered in the following year. Later the already much damaged castle was further reduced to render it useless in further conflict. In truth, one of the ruins Cromwell knocked about a bit.

Incredibly it was left to decay for a full 200 years, until members of the Dent family (the famous glovers of Worcester) took a hand, with a programme of rescue and restoration of both castle and church. That work continues today in the hands of the present owners.

Visitors making their way round the house will take away differing impressions, maybe they will recall a particular painting but it is in the church that the historical connections come to life. Sun streaming through the windows, dust dancing in the shafts of light that throw a pool of colour on the floor. The eye travels back up the beam to find the colours coalescing into the portraits in the stained glass windows of people associated with Sudeley whose names read like the index of Who's Who in English history.

Henry VIII, standing four square, instantly recognisable to all, a strong, vigorous ruler, whose thirty-eight year reign has produced more historical studies and dramas than probably any other. A time of enormous change and with powerful advisers like Wolsey and Cromwell at his right hand, both of their careers ending with charges of treason. His desperate need to father a male successor taking him through six marriage ceremonies. His last wife, Katherine Parr, survived Henry, and within the year of his death married the Lord High Admiral of England, Thomas Seymour, Baron Sudeley. All three are seen in the same window.

It was a short marriage, Katherine died soon after giving birth to a daughter. Her tomb is near the altar, the inscription reads: "Here lies Queen Katherine, wife of Henry VIII and last." She was a devout woman, in the castle two of her books are on display, "Lamentations of a sinner" and "Prayers of meditation."

Seymour's elder brother, Edward, was Lord Protector of England under the young King Edward. The two were in conflict, and in 1549 Thomas was beheaded. A similar fate awaited Edward, his days of office were numbered and in January 1552 he too fell to the executioner's axe.

Another window commemorates Miles Coverdale, chaplain to Katherine while at Sudeley and remembered as one of the early translators of the Bible. We see him with quill and bible in hand with his Bishop's mitre and crook at his feet. Lady Jane Grey lived for a time at Sudeley. Jane was the grand-daughter of Henry VIIIs sister, Mary. Her marriage to Lord Dudley was another strand in the many political plots of the period. There was an attempt to put her on the throne, she and her husband suffered the inevitable consequences. Next to Lady Jane, we find the first Lord Chandos, he and his family were to be connected with Sudeley for the hundred years following his elevation to the title in 1554.

The story which the windows tell continues: another shows the young martyr, St. Kenelm and his father King Kenulf, with the Abbey that he founded at Winchcombe in his hand.

Among the varying attractions are occasional falconry demonstrations and the formal gardens which are a delight.

The Walk, continued

On reaching the road turn left into Winchcombe and then right on the Broadway/Stratford road. There is a "Pilgrims House" and a "Pilgrims Progress," to remind us of past travellers along this way. The George Inn, dating back to about 1450 is said to have catered to their needs.

Soon after crossing the river at the edge of the town, take the path on the right, Puck Pitt Lane, following the waymarked Cotswold Way back to Hailes. After a while the broad track is lost but the route is well-marked over the fields. When a road is reached (Salters Lane) turn right and in a short distance join the broad track on the left, the waymark will be seen on the side of a house. Soon the track gives way to a field path which is followed to meet the road by Hailes Abbey.

The Capital of Wincelcumbeshire: a guide to Winchcombe

It is not a profitable exercise to seek out the county of Wincelcumbeshire on a modern map, or to similarly locate the one time capital of Mercia. Despite the omission in this form by modern cartographers it was an important place, and a street map of the day would have included the royal palace, a mint, nunnery, a castle and an Abbey founded by a king.

The reader may by now have concluded that at this point in our exploration of the western Cotswolds we have arrived at the ancient Saxon Borough of Winchcombe. Today's visitor will look in vain for a royal standard announcing that the king is in residence. Any manufacture of the coin of the realm will be unofficial, and if any monks are to be seen walking the streets they will be from the modern monastery of Prinknash or ghosts from the past.

This is not to say that Winchcombe is a dead town. Far from it, and you will be in some difficulty if you trt to combine a look at Winchcombe with a day's walking. If time allows it is worth while to allocate a day and twin a leisurely exploration of Winchcombe with a visit to Sudeley Castle. Its location may also commend it as a centre for touring the area for it is beautifully placed beneath the shelter of the wooded hills and convenient for excursions in several directions. The many old buildings contrive to make Winchcombe, not a polished show-case exhibit, but a down to earth, homely and comfortable town.

In its day it has been a place of royal patronage, of religious devotion and pilgrimage, an industrious wool town, to say nothing of a shady past as a centre for an illegal industry. It has enjoyed the privileges of power, the prosperity of progress, suffered the poverty of decline and the pillage and plunder of warring factions.

Where better to start than the Town Hall, for here is not only the Tourist Information Office but also two museums. The first, surprisingly for a small Gloucestershire town, is the Simm's International Police Collection. Here are the results of thirty-five years spent collecting memorabilia by one man, Ross Simms, a former Scotland Yard officer.

Included in the world's largest assembly of police uniforms is the every day wear of the Bow Street Runner. Forerunner of today's constable he is seen with tricorn hat, single breasted jacket, frock coat, breeches and stockings, his wardrobe completed by a neck tie and lace edge scarf. The WPC of 1924 was fashionably dressed in calf length skirt meeting her lace up boots, high necked tunic, and a bowler type hat.

Headgear has always been an important part of the uniform, adding that extra stamp of authority. Apart from our own familiar helmets there are helmets and caps from Switzerland, Italy, Australia and the Nazi police of 1937. The badges of office range from a collection of county cap badges to a Sheriff's badge from New Orleans, and the California Highway Patrol badge made familiar by a thousand imported television police dramas.

Truncheons are not unexpectedly featured, among them a Kenyan riot stick. Associated equipment includes a bull's eye lamp of 1840, a long barrelled naval colt issued to the Thames River Police and chemical mace used by some forces in the US.

Only a few steps away mace takes on a different, more peaceful, meaning, for in the folk museum is the seal and mace of sixteenth century Winchcombe. A small but varied collection has some contrasting items, a musket ball from the early 15th century and a Spitfire cannon shell. There are various household, trade and farm tools and shepherd's smock – but there is one item that is almost certain to raise a wry smile. It is a notice convening a meeting of the inhabitants of Winchcombe and vicinity ". . . in order to take into consideration, what, if anything, can be done to improve local postal services." It is dated 23rd May, 1824.

All this evidence of the sharp end of the administration of justice is taken a step further just outside the Town Hall where the familiar stocks remain. Unless you are specially observant you may fail to notice anything unusual about this particular instrument of public punishment. If you count the leg holes, you will find that there are seven, when you might have expected to have found an even number. The story goes that one local villain, who was evidently a regular customer for the forces of law and order in the distant past, was short of a leg. (Was he the town drunk and therefore habitually legless I wondered?).

Some people, according to Rose Fyleman, have fairies at the bottom of the garden, others prefer gnomes, but at 23 Gloucester Street, they do things differently. They have a railway museum. From between the lettuces and strawberries tall signal gantries rise, the red poppies in the flower beds echoing the lights set at danger. You don't have to be a railway buff to enjoy this museum. There are items of railway interest from all parts of Britain, some dating as far back as 1799 and no less than five hundred railways are represented in one form or another. Long forgotten companies like Oldham, Ashton and Guide Bridge Railway, Shropshire Union Railway and Canal Company, or the Rhondda and Swansea Bay, Lancashire and Yorkshire, the South Eastern and Chatham Railway Companies. Their names are legion to say nothing of the more famous Great Western and its rivals, all are remembered in some fashion, by ticket or tablet, by brass button or iron insignia.

This remembrance of the age of steam and smut is recalled in many different ways. There is a huge collection of cast iron plates designed to inform and warn both passengers and staff. Signs from long dead stations, Devizes for instance, engine numbers . . . the collectors delight even today. Dozens of do's and don'ts: from warnings to unwary passengers not to cross the line, to a threat issued in the Victorian age, of prosecution to those caught throwing stones at telegraphs.

There are the familiar furnishings of the station, porters' barrows, fire buckets, old enamelled advertising plates for products still famous today and others now in oblivion. Much of this is out in the open with hens and ducks foraging. Close to the tracks and beyond the trees, the tower of St. Peter's church completes the rural scene.

Under cover the collection continues with a myriad of items, an

The Railway Museum, Winchcombe

array of railway uniform buttons and insignia . . . all ages . . . all ranks. There is crockery and cutlery, all proudly inscribed with the operating company's name. Uniforms, lanterns, whistles and steam pressure gauges and railway clocks. Railway clocks, now that is a romantic notion, how many adventures have started with a meeting under the clock on platform one? The passenger's comfort is not forgotten, there are fire boxes and stoves from waiting rooms and those delightful nostalgic pictures of desirable seaside resorts in water colours.

Naturally there is a Booking Office, complete with tickets, stamping machine and of course a kettle in the corner. There is much more but the beautifully equipped signal box can't be left unmentioned and there is no bar on trying your strength on its great levers.

There is no doubt that work on the railway was long and hard. Yet those thundering, hissing, roaring giants of the iron road produced a sense of romance and adventure in travel that is now largely absent. This museum recalls it all – don't miss it. But then that would be difficult because if you walk down Gloucester Street in Winchcombe number twenty three has a house number that is unique . . . a L.M.S. & G.W. Joint Railway plate.

Propped against a wall in St. Peter's Church is an old door bearing the initials R.K., elsewhere there are two ancient stone coffins. In a convoluted way these items are chapter headings in the story of the long lost Abbey of Winchcombe, founded by one king and destroyed seven centuries later by another. R.K. was Richard Kidderminster, or Kyderminster, almost the last Abbot of Winchcombe. The coffins are those of King Kenulf of Mercia, who founded the Abbey in 811 within which was a shrine dedicated to his son, Kenelm.

Richard was a scholarly man and enhanced the abbey as a seat of learning. The head of an important and successful religious foundation would have much to occupy his attention but despite these demands he was not the man to sit in his own backyard. However busy the activities of the Abbey might have kept him, he was also involved in the politics of the day. Regularly attending Parliament and we hear of him as an emissary to the Papal court.

It is the story of the young saint Kenelm that is the strangest. Even allowing for the fantasies that still linger on from the past, and presumably less enlightened ages, it is one that must have stretched the credulity of even the most gullible of the population, accustomed as they were to the belief in the darker doings of witchcraft and the like. It is the stuff of greed and lust for power that has filled the pages of history and which served Shakespeare so well in his historical plays. Whilst one may choose to assume that the legend is built upon some grains of truth, the exotic embroidery that surrounds it serves only to place a heavy disguise on the basic structure of the story. The laboured symbolism of some of the features and the cliche ridden plot will soon become apparent.

The dramatis personae are Kenulf (or Ceonwulf according to the spelling you prefer) a Mercian King, his seven-year-old son, Kenelm and his wicked sister Quendrida, the Pope, the monks of Winchcombe, a white dove, and in some versions of the story, a white cow.

Act one would read something like this, Kenulf in his wisdom (or lack of it) sends his seven-year-old son and heir to his elder sister in order to further his education. Quendrida is an ambitious woman with aspirations to the throne and upon the death of Kenulf conspires with the prince's tutor to arrange the boy's murder. This takes place in a lonely spot in the Clent Hills of Worcestershire where the innocent Kenelm has been lured by the subterfuge of a hunting trip. Thus far we have Shakespeare's attention for the story as a possible vehicle for another big hit at the Globe. From hereon we may assume that the bard's enthusiasm might wane.

Act two has a dove rising from the headless body of the slaughtered child and flying off to Rome to acquaint the Pope with the news of the dastardly deed. The monks of Winchcombe are alerted and set out to find the secret grave of the young king (or prince as the case may be). They are aided in their search by a white cow.

In Act three the monks return to Winchcombe and build a shrine within the Abbey where they intend to bury Kenelm alongside his father. On the return journey another miracle takes place, the body rests overnight on the slopes of Sudeley Hill and a spring of healing water gushes forth. In the next scene a long and solemn procession makes its way past the royal palace for the entombment. Now witchcraft takes a hand. Quendrida enraged at the discovery of the young prince's body and the reverence accorded to the martyr attempts to put a curse upon the proceedings by reciting Psalm 109 backwards. (It is not exactly full of joy and goodwill read the right way round.) This has a dramatic effect, but not the one intended, the tables are turned and the wicked aunt's eyes are torn from her head and she perishes in a welter of blood.

Act four, or the transformation scene, completes the drama with a representation of the pilgrimage to Winchcombe and the shrine that continued for several centuries. Whatever one chooses to make of these stories, the fact remains that there was a long history of pilgrimage to the shrine of Kenelm. His well is still marked on today's OS maps and two coffins, obviously of persons of importance are preserved within the church.

Close by the door of Richards Abbey is another fragment from the past, an altar cloth believed to have been embroidered, in part, by Catherine of Aragon, first wife of Henry VIII. Her badge, a pomegranate is sewn into the border. There is a strange coincidence attached to the altar cloth, it was long in use in the church but from 1872 it was displayed at Sudeley Castle. On its return to the church in 1928 it was sent to the experts at the Royal School of Needlework for restoration. By a curious chance a similar piece of work from Minsterworth was also in Kensington for repair. It was discovered that a section of the Winchcombe panel, part of the crucifixion, was incorporated in their cloth

Another curiosity is a pillar collecting box dated 1547. It is equipped with three separate locks which worked independently so that offerings for the poor could only be recovered in the presence of the vicar and both church wardens. There is a similar box in the old Broadway church. There must have been some common problems associated with the collection of money to be administered by the church at that time for this three-way security to have been found necessary. There is also a handsome parish chest, nine feet long. Within it is an earlier chest dating back to the 12th century, which had been made by hollowing out the trunk of an oak tree.

All these items are seen as the church is explored but the immediate impression the visitor receives is of a fine airy church, the high windows bathing the interior of the building with light. One instinctively looks down the nave to the chancel and the attention is taken at once by the seven panelled window above the altar. Rich in design and colour it depicts the scene described in Matthew Chapter 14 where Christ and Peter walk upon the water and the storm is stilled. In addition to the full complement of the disciples angels seem to have taken over the fishing duties at fore and aft.

Within the chancel kneels a lonely man, Sir Thomas Williams. His handsome monument shows him at prayer by a double sided reading desk. The space opposite is empty, clearly it was intended that his wife should join him in his final devotions, but he has been there, sadly alone, for these past three hundred and fifty years. Alas his widow married another, will they be reunited at the last trump? A problem of Solomon proportions to engage the legal mind of this former judge.

Externally the church is decorated, if that's the word, with a collection of gargoyles, which look malevolently down upon all who pass below, more of a warning than a welcome you might suppose. Here the masons have allowed their imaginations full play, in competition perhaps to see who could sculpt the most hideous and frightening head.

Winchcombe's many old and pleasing buildings will have their own stories to tell, and at least one is reputed to be haunted, the oddly named Old Corner Cupboard Inn. Equally oddly named is Rabbit Box House, it has been suggested that the stone work showing the rabbit now incorporated in the buildings may once have been part of the Abbey.

Myths and legends apart, Winchcombe's most unlikely past is connected with a period of illegal prosperity. Nothing to do with the populace taking a leaf out of the Saxon Mint's book, but another form of private enterprise. It is not difficult to see that wealth accrued to the town from its close association with the Abbey and the spin off from the pilgrimages. In common with other Cotswold towns and villages it shared in the long settled period of a comfortable economy founded on the woollen industry, and later the rearing of sheep with more emphasis on the market value of the meat. These sources of income lasted for centuries. Rather more short lived was a thriving industry that was destined, however you care to look at it, to go up in smoke.

The exploration of America and the West Indies led to a large tobacco industry in the colonies, one which the government of the day was anxious to support and it became illegal to grow the crop in this country. This restriction did not unduly trouble the people of Gloucestershire who knew a good thing when they saw it. John Stratford, local born in the Manor House at Farmcote who, like another son of Gloucestershire before him, a certain Richard Whittington, left home to make his fortune in London. He became a successful trader and in scenting the profits to be made out of the fast increasing smoking of tobacco, developed the growing and processing of the crop in and around Winchcombe. It was a considerable success and Stratford prospered greatly for a time by the substantial undercutting of the price of the imported, but superior product.

Stratford and his fellow growers were of course treading upon tender toes and more than one attempt was made by London to put an end to the industry. But they were not easily effected, with the capital so far away and those locally responsible for law and order prepared to turn a blind eye. On occasions in the 1650s and 1660s the population turned out in force to resist armed troops who had been ordered in the county to fire the crop. In course of time the tobacco industry which had enjoyed a vogue for perhaps fifty years faded away, as much perhaps due to the climate and uncertain harvests as to the enforcement tactics of the government.

Walk 7: Shades of The Past

Belas Knap and a ghost story

Route: Winchcombe – Wadfield – Belas Knap – Cleeve Common – Postlip – Winchcombe

Map: 1:50,000 Landranger Sheet 163, 1:25,000 Pathfinder 1067 (SP 02/12) 1066 (SO 82/92)

Distance: 8 miles

Parking: Near Winchcombe library off Back Lane

Toilets: Winchcombe, corner of Vineyard Street

The Walk

From the car park by the library take the signed path to the town centre via Cowl Lane which passes along the edge of the former Abbey grounds. Turn right along Abbey Terrace and after a short distance turn left on the road signed to Sudeley Castle. This is Vineyard Street, with a delightful row of cottages, some with roses round the door. Locally this has been known as Duck Lane, not the roast and orange sauce variety, but a reference to the practice of ducking sharp-tongued women, scolds, in the little River Isbourne which is soon crossed. Just before the driveway to the castle is reached, bear right on the Cotswold Way and follow a No Through Road which edges the castle grounds.

After about 250 yards, the Cotswold Way is signed off right, through a kissing gate. The path heads diagonally across a field with a large footpath sign on a telegraph post to remove any uncertainty. After that, there are several fields to be crossed, all well waymarked, and a steady upward progress is made to Wadfield Farm, with retrospective views of Winchcombe tucked beneath the hills and to Sudeley Castle.

Wadfield House is reached about a mile after leaving the road, a handsome, square building, with croquet lawn and wrought iron gates set to the field edge.

'Wad' is thought to be a corruption of 'woad', the plant from

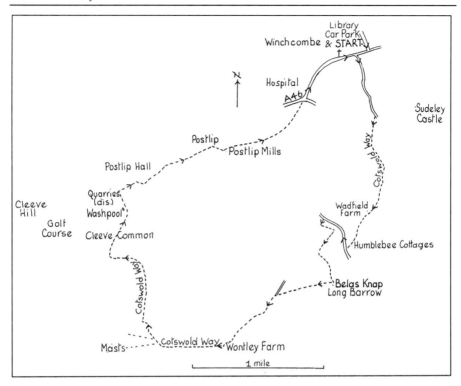

which the ancient Britons extracted the dye with which to smear their bodies in the hope of striking fear into the hearts of their enemies. In more recent times the dye was used in the production of police uniforms. We are close to the heart of the former Cotswold cloth industry, so it may be that woad commercially grown here was supplied to the dyers of Stroud and Uley before the chemical processes took over.

The walk continues, passing Wadfield House on your right, soon the path widens and rises towards the prettily-named Humblebee Cottages.

The map notes the site of another Roman villa, but this is off our path. The views are good in gentle walking country, with farm tracks running through the fields to the summits, with many mature trees, particularly ash and oak to add interest to the landscape.

The path divides at the cottages, take the right fork, passing the ancient bicycle wheel set into the gate of one of them. After a short distance the road is reached, Corndean Lane, here turn right and follow it for just under half a mile as it terraces the hillside. In season, the wayside is patriotically decorated in the red, white and blue colours of poppy, elder flower, and mallow. Blackberries promise a free snack to walkers passing this way in late summer.

A road sign threatens a 1 in 5 descent and just before the lane swoops down the hill, Belas Knap and Cleeve Common are signed off to the left. From the road cross a stile and follow the path as it climbs steeply through a wooded section. After passing through a kissing gate turn left and follow a level path with the wood to your left. At the field end bear right, as signed, and continue uphill.

The views are again improving, with Winchcombe cupped within the bosom of the hills. At the top of the hill pass through a further kissing gate and continue with a dry stone wall on your left. The distant Sudeley Castle can be seen over the wall. First built before the considerations of artillery attack had to be taken into account, it presents a clear target for the gunnery spotter.

The path now follows the edge of a wood stretching across Humblebee How. As a bend in the path is rounded, the hump of Belas Knap long barrow comes into view. Since leaving Winchcombe some 700 feet of height have been gained, the long barrow being 960 feet above sea level.

Belas Knap

It is an impressive monument with its shape resembling a stranded whale with the ground plan not unlike a two-toed foot. The barrow is one of a number in the region, which archaeologists have labelled together under the title Severn-Cotswold Group. We will meet other examples as our walking extends further south. The barrow is about 180 feet long, 60 feet wide and 18 feet in height. There are four separate burial chambers, and a central circle of stones. Dry stone walling and standing stones have been used in constructing the barrow, which dates from about 3000BC. This was in the Neolithic (new stone age) period, when man was settling down to clear the forests, farm both crops and livestock on the land, and develop the use of stone implements. It represented the growth of more settled, and probably larger, communities than the earlier nomadic hunters who had hitherto inhabited Britain. To put Belas Knap into a historical context, it can be said that it is very roughly contemporary with the earliest parts of Stonehenge.

By stooping low, or crawling on hands and knees, it is possible to scramble through the low passages into the small burial chambers. This is a mild adventure, with photographic opportunities for shots looking out from the darkness of the tomb. Slightly more dramatic pictures can be produced from within Hetty Pegler's Tump at Uley, which is visited later.

In addition to the burial chambers, a false entrance was constructed at the northern end of the barrow, to mislead grave robbers. The building of the barrow would have involved a considerable use of man power. Labour, which would have to have been diverted from the everyday business of living, when much of mans energy must have been devoted to survival.

Despite its size only 38 skeletons have been discovered and it seems fair to assume that these substantial monuments must have been reserved for people of importance. Whatever the ceremonies that accompanied the entombment of these community leaders or local chieftains, there was no great treasure trove of riches buried with them, or left to satisfy our curiosity today. Just some fragments of pottery, a bone scraper, a boar's tusk, a bone or two and items from a later period have been uncovered.

In an age when life was short and time doubly precious, they built well in honour of their dead and perhaps in pursuit of (to us,) an unknown religion. Even so, they should merit our respect, for these stone age men led the way into farming, trading and eventually industry. Certainly they are undeserving of the unthinking vandalism of the twentieth century that left the remains of a burnt-out fire and several beer cans at the now scorched false portal.

From the barrow the path heads westward along the field edges on the

flat summit top. At the end of the prairie-sized field our route joins a farm track heading south-westerly and in half a mile reaches Wontley Farm. Here a long line of pylons marches relentlessly across the landscape, a chain gang of giant robots. From the farm take the broad uphill track on the right. As the rise is topped, the radio-masts again come into view almost directly ahead. Soon the cultivated land gives way to the semi-moorland of Cleeve Common. There has been a diversion from the original route of the Cotswold Way, which has been in place for some years now and is carefully posted throughout. At the metal gate on the Common edge the paths divide. Take the right fork and follow the Cotswold Way over the open hillside keeping your eye open for the marker posts signing the changes of direction. The way makes a slightly curving progress, roughly northwards. After about three-quarters of a mile it descends into a deep cleft with the radio-masts high to the south. The banks on either side of the path are favoured by orchids. The next walk also covers part of this area – see this for orchid detail.

The deep ravine-like incision owes something to both man and nature, as the path falls into it turn right and continue with the Cotswold Way through old quarries. A spring appears and then the Washpool that sends water tumbling down the hillside. Keep to the left of the stream and still on the Cotswold Way go forward for about 300 yards until a small coppice is reached.

At this point abandon the Cotswold Way, the waymarking will now be without the identifying white spot. A yellow waymarked stile on the right takes you through the coppice and on through a field. After passing through metal gates, a track is reached edged by the high stone wall of Postlip Hall. Turn right along the track with the wall on your left and farm buildings on the right. After a few yards pass through another gate, cross a farm track and continue forward with the wall still on your left. Go through a wooden gate into a field, still following the line of the wall.

At the end of the wall, go through yet another metal gate and continue on the yellow waymarked path with a tiny stream on your left. The path is a little overgrown here and there and the stream disappears from view behind thick hedges. About half a mile after leaving the Hall wall, and just before a bridleway, cross a stream by a small bridge. The turn is waymarked on a willow tree but easily missed. Once over the stream turn right and after a few yards bear left on a broad track. After the quiet of the countryside, you are suddenly plunged into a hive of activity, for ahead is the Postlip Mill.

Broad Track to Wontley Farm

Postlip Mills

Watermills have been a source of power for at least two thousand years and are believed to have existed in Britain from Roman times. By the time William the Conqueror's tax surveyors were at work on the Domesday Book there were thousands of water-mills to be recorded, many of them in Gloucestershire.

Rivers large and small lent themselves to the production of power for grinding corn. Often aided by the diversion of water through specially constructed mill streams or heads of water held in mill pond reservoirs. As industry progressed the power was used for other purposes, fulling woven cloth, grinding ore, paper making and the rather more hazardous production of gunpowder.

The little River Isbourne powered a number of mills along its course, with continuity at Postlip since Saxon times. Initially they ground corn but there is evidence of a paper industry in Gloucestershire for at least three hundred and fifty years, aided by the plentiful supply of fresh clean water, a major ingredient in production. On the walk described in chapter five the route passed close to Papermill Farm. Paper was being produced in Stanway by 1635 and probably earlier, but there does not appear to be a precise date for the start of production at Postlip.

John Durham steps into the story. After serving his apprentice-ship, he was active in Winchcombe as a paper manufacturer on his own account by 1725. This at least is a firm date in the history of paper production at Postlip. In those early days hand-made paper was produced and beautifully watermarked. The company still have several of the wire rollers, some dating back to around 1730.

By 1807 the business was owned by Joseph Lloyd and his three brothers. In 1826, new machinery was in use at Postlip. There were several changes in ownership, notably the partnership from the middle of the nineteenth century of James Evans, William Adlard and William Gilling. They were then employing 20 men and 32 women. Production methods continued to improve and by 1870 the work force had multiplied threefold.

Evans Adlard was long respected in the industry, and although no longer a family business the name survives as part of the American based company, Hollingsworth and Vose. People have changed and the product has also. Blotting paper for example is no longer an essential item in the modern office or school. Today's manufacture is concentrated on the highly specialised area of filter papers, widely used in the motor, oil and food industries as well as in health care.

The public footpath passes through the Mill grounds, and is waymarked on various buildings. Go forward through the car park, then left, past the building with the flagpoles, continuing through the works-complex. Ignore the path signed to Corndean Farm that appears at the end of the loading bay and continue with the stream on your right. A concrete road gives way to a track. As this bends left, take the waymarked path on the right. Follow this over the fields for nearly half a mile to reach the road at the corner of Corndean Lane. Go forward to join the main road by Winchcombe Hospital and continue into the town. En route you will pass Tobacco Close, marking a site of the industry that flourished here in the seventeenth century, and the Old Corner Cupboard Inn, dating from the thirteenth century and originally a farm house.

The Old Corner Cupboard Inn

Most ghost stories centre on unhappy events, sudden death, grief stricken lovers, walled up nuns and the like. The Corner Cupboard Inn is an exception, since there is no background story nor any indication of who the ghost may be, or even that she is in anyway unhappy.

She is from the Victorian era, a young girl, about ten years old, wearing a long blue dress so perhaps we may be allowed to call her Alice. She is said to appear under an arch at midday. Then she walks up a flight of stairs from the original farm house, before making herself comfortable in a rocking chair. The creaking of the chair is then heard as Alice rocks gently back and forth. In a building as old as the Inn the creaking sound is not difficult to believe. There do not appear to have been any recent sightings but I am told that two ladies, now quite elderly, claim to have seen Alice some years ago. The Inn was run by the Richardson family from 1850 until 1952 but the ghost is not known to be one of their relatives. So we are left with a real mystery. Who was Alice, where did she come from and why is a person of her tender years to be seen in the Inn?

The inn boasts a refreshingly unusual name but there is no mystery how it came by it. Apparently it stems from the intro-duction of the tobacco tax. It was the practice for inns to give away free pipes with the tobacco they sold, and it became a requirement that these were stamped with the names of the inn. Up until then it was nameless, being one of several ale houses in the town. The Landlady being called upon to give the name for stamping on the pipes, responded, apparently on the spur of the moment, with "The Old Corner Cupboard" since, there were several remaining from its farmhouse days. There are still two of these cupboards in the public bar.

Rabbit House is seen on the right and the Railway Museum on the left, and close to the church, the old school.

A fading tablet records its foundation 120 years ago. "This school was endowed at the bequest of John Dent (the glover), formerly a citizen of Worcester and Lord of the Manor of Winchcombe and Sudeley." The school was opened in January 1868, the founda-tion stone being laid with this prayer:

"May God bless this school that is now about to be built to His honour and glory. May all the boys and girls of Winchcombe learn to fear God and honour the King and in every respect to live as the good founder of this school would have wished them to do."

John Dent was a member of a family who were benefactors in several ways to the town of Winchcombe, including the alms houses in Dent Terrace.

Continue past the church and left into Cowl Lane to return to your starting point.

Walk 8: Top of The Lot

Cleeve Hill

Route: Cleeve Hill Club House — summit — Cleeve Cloud — Cotswold Way to old quarries — West Down — Wontley Farm — Cleeve Common

Map: 1:50,000 Landranger Sheet 163, 1:25,000 Pathfinder 1066 (SO82/92), 1067 (SP02/12)

Distance: 8 miles

Parking: Golf-course, signed off the B4632 at Woodmancote, parking beyond club house in old quarry

Toilets: B4632 by Cleeve Lodge stables

Cleeve Hill and Cleeve Common

Mountains are in short supply in Gloucestershire but it is well-endowed with some splendid hills, notably where the high ground of the Cotswolds drops, often sharply, into the valleys. Cleeve Hill at 1085 feet, is the highest point, celebrated by the Cheltenham Rotary Club, in conjunction with its Jubilee, by the installation of a topograph.

There is evidence of man's past occupation of this high common with hut circles identified within the banks of the fort on Cleeve Cloud. There is another bank and ditch circle known as The Ring and, a little south of the summit, Cross Dyke runs east to west over the hill, thought to be an old boundary marker. Our route passes a not very exciting rock, known as Huddlestone's Table. There are several abandoned quarries scattered throughout the area, nature reclaiming its own, and creating a habitat that both animals and birds are quick to turn to their advantage.

The marks of man are not confined to the past. Three radio-masts thrust to the sky like a modern calvary and a golf course is spread over the summit plateau, encroaching upon the earthworks of two

Deep in a cleft of Cleeve Hill

thousand years ago. The golfers may have a marvellous view but have to pay for the pleasure by the acquisition of the extra skill needed to cope with the vagaries of the wind.

The Walk

From the car park take the path running south that edges the golf course. In about a quarter of a mile, near Cleeve Lodge Racing Stables, take the track that runs half-left uphill. As the way levels out, take the path half left towards the summit and note ahead a post with the familiar Cotswold Way marking. At the post, bear right to the top of the hill. The minor twists and turns to the summit are all waymarked.

The views improve as height is gained. Soon you are at eye level with the summit of Nottingham Hill to the west, and the nine mile run of the Malvern Hills making their rolling progress along the skyline. Ahead can be seen Cheltenham's famous race-course. Soon the Rotary Club's topograph is helping you to pick out the landmarks. Tewkesbury Abbey can be identified and beyond, the Herefordshire Beacon, better known as the British Camp. The white tip of Gloucester Cathedral eleven miles away may be seen. Leckhampton Hill and Painswick Beacon are to the south, both calling places on later walks.

It is a magnificent view, and walking along the scarp on a day of sunshine and showers it is not only the scenery that can be enjoyed but the ever changing skyscape. Racing clouds, white, grey and black driven by a stiff breeze and you may watch the sharp shower that falls upon Cheltenham or the rainbow arching over Winchcombe.

From the summit the way heads roughly south, passing by greens and occasionally meeting golfers searching in the rough for lost balls that are casualties of the high wind. The manicured greens are in sharp contrast with the free growth intended by nature. Her wild garden is sown with handsome, brightly-flowered thistles, yellow gorse and here and there little spikes of bugle.

Having passed through the remains of the fort the track heads towards the wireless masts, but soon veers as a blue arrow and a white spot are seen on the right at the edge of the common by a notice board. The

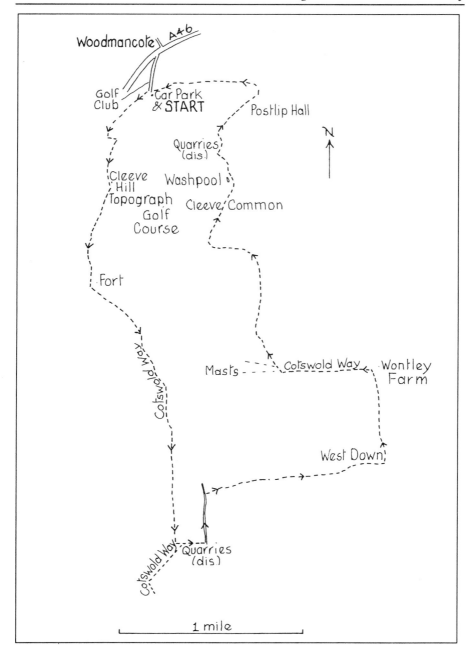

bridleway would be confusing but for the waymarking, for there is a maze of crossing paths. This keeps you on course as you pass under the lee of the hill with the masts high above.

When a deep gullied path is reached, turn left uphill. After a short distance bear to the right and cross a five-barred gate, with wood on your left, maintaining your direction for just under a mile. After a while you are lost to the world as the path makes its way through a cleft in the hills. The way is lined with hawthorn, tangled with dog rose and wild hops, with meadowsweet at the base. But the world, and Cheltenham in particular is again returned to view. A junction of paths is reached at an old quarry and this is where we part company with the Cotswold Way.

Join the left path, which is followed for 350 yards, until a lane is reached opposite the track to Dry Pool Farm. Turn left up the lane for just over a quarter of a mile then take the broad track on the right, which is followed for about a mile to reach West Down.

From West Down take the good track, which runs northwards to reach, in half a mile, Wontley Farm, rejoining the course of the Cotswold Way. As the farm is reached, turn left, still on the broad track, which is followed to the gated entrance to Cleeve Common.

Here, follow the waymarked route over the common running roughly northwards. There are views to Winchcombe in the valley and Sudeley Castle on the rising ground beyond. The path drops down to a deep cleft in the hills and turns right to pass through the old quarries.

Hereabouts several varieties of orchid are to be found, among them common spotted, pyramidal and bee orchids. Orchids sound far too exotic to be found in the British countryside. Certainly it is a far cry from the delicate pampered flower so carefully tended under glass, or the fantastic tree climbers of tropical forests. Nevertheless there are over fifty varieties to be found in this country, some so rare that they are limited to one or two sites. Unless you are an expert you will need help in identification and the Field Guide to Orchids of Britain and Europe, published by Collins, will be found useful.

Orchids may be discovered in many places; woods, pastures, quarries, heathlands, sand dunes or along hedgerows according to variety. They range in size from a few inches to over three feet.

Some varieties like chalk or limestone country so that many flourish in places like the Cotswolds, Chiltern and the South Downs. Often they have interesting names or habits. The Bee Orchid is said to encourage pollination by its resemblance to a female bee. Ladies' Tresses speaks for itself as does the Lady Slipper. There are a man orchid, a frog orchid, a monkey orchid and a military orchid. These last two are rare.

Continue with the Cotswold Way, through the old quarries, passing the Washpool and on to a clump of trees, which is reached in about 300 yards. Here the Way climbs the hill bearing half left and identified by posts. Just before the summit is reached, abandon the Cotswold Way to turn right on a broad track. Follow it along the edge of the golf course until another track is found. Turn left with this, again following the edge of the course to return to your starting point, passing the paddocks of a racing stable en route.

Walk 9: A Hill, A Horse and A Heart

The Devil's Chimney and Seven Springs

Route: Seven Springs — Hartley Hill — Leckhampton Hill — Devil's Chimney — Hartley Wood — Coberley — Seven Springs

Map: 1:50,000 Landranger sheet 163, 1:25,000 Pathfinder 1089 (SO 81/91)

Distance: 5 miles

Parking: Seven Springs, lay-by on A436, just short of the junction with A435

The walk starts from the lay-by almost opposite Seven Springs Hotel and begins with a long running dispute.

Seven Springs

Here just off a busy road is what must pass in England for an oasis, surrounded not by date palms but by good English beech trees. Cool clear water rises to the surface from, as the name suggests, seven springs. No doubt at least half the people who visit this spot feel obliged to verify the accuracy of the name, and probably make it six at the first count. A stone let in the wall bears a Latin inscription:

> Hic Tuus
> O Tamesine Pater
> Septemceminus Fons

Roughly translated this reads: Here is your sevenfold spring fount, O Father Thames. The claim that this is the source of the River Thames is based on it being the source of the River Churn, its highest tributary. The generally accepted source is Thames Head, near Cirencester.

The Walk

Leave the layby and turn left to follow the busy A436 to meet the junction with the A435. A little building on the right may catch your eye, this is the

Parcel House, and was used for the deposit and collection of items into this century. At the junction turn left and, just past the AA box, take the lane on the left signed Cotswold Way. The lane rises steadily, edged with scabious, wild pansy, white campion, knapweed and a generous scattering of poppies in the fields. In a little under half a mile the lane makes a sharp turn left to Hartley Farm, but our route pushes forward signed to Leckhampton Hill. The Cotswold Way continues as a wide track, which is muddy in places. At a dip, where a more-or-less permanent pool has formed, the prospect of wet feet is avoided by the provision of a little bridge.

After the water-splash the Way bends to the left at a cross road of paths and soon emerges into a large rectangular field. This is followed uphill to

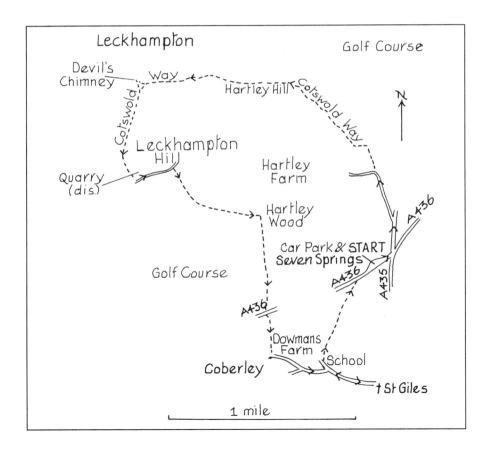

the top corner, then along its top side with thick hedgerows on the left. At the far end of the field turn left through a short wooded section.

Once through the trees the Way climbs steadily in a hollow way. After rain this is rather greasy and is a trap for the unwary. The path quickly improves and follows the edge of the scarp with a steep drop to the right. You are high above a golf course, where mini figures, those other long distance walkers, take their exercise on smoother ground, no rucksacks, their burdens conveyed on golf trolleys.

As the path edges Hartley Hill, Cheltenham comes into view and the ground, undisturbed by the plough offers a variety of wild flowers attracting numbers of colourful butterflies. Keep with the path along the edge of the scarp, any uncertainties being resolved by waymarking. When some long-disused quarries are reached, the path curves to the left through a more wooded section. Once out of the quarry area, pass the triangulation point away to the left, which marks the summit at 962 feet. Cross the open the hill top within the circlet of the earthworks of a fort, to reach further old quarries. At this point the Cotswold Way swings left. Leave it for the moment and turn right to visit the Devil's Chimney.

Devil's Chimney

The chimney owes more to the work of man than to the machinations of Satan. However, the local story is in keeping with the best traditions of ascribing supernatural origins to events and places. It is baldly stated that the chimney rises straight from Hell. If so, they must be having a very quiet time down there. Failing that, we are left with the assumption that the local authority has contrived to serve a smoke control order on the nether regions.

The fifty-foot high column has an interesting shape, a modern sculpture if you like, that would not be out of place in a civic park with a famous name inscribed at its base. Long may it remain where it is, adding a little touch of the spectacular to a landscape already made more dramatic by the quarrymen's activities. You actually look down upon the chimney from this point and some scrambling is called for to get into a position for a photograph that will make the right impression.

After inspecting the Devil's Chimney and the wide views, retrace your

Bridging the gap on the Cotswold Way near Seven Springs

steps to rejoin the Cotswold Way, which is followed southwards for about half a mile until yet another abandoned quarry is reached. Follow the edge of the quarry (on your right) to meet a lane and turn left, still with the Cotswold Way. In about 300 yards, just before a white house is reached, take the path on the right.

We now leave the Cotswold Way and take the path signposted Coberley. As now used this is not exactly as shown on some maps. Take the direction signed and follow the field boundaries to your left for about three-quarters of a mile to join the north-south path at the outer edge of Hartley Wood. Here turn right, south, with the wood on your left. When the summit of the small rise is reached a line of trees on the opposite hillside is seen standing up like targets at a shooting gallery. The path widens into a track, a little overgrown and luxuriant with wild flowers, scabious, willow herb, cranesbill and not short of thistles. A high-contrast with the billiard table smoothness of the golf course beyond the fence.

When a road is reached (the A436 — this point is just over half a mile from Seven Springs) take the path almost opposite signed to Coberley. This path leads south to Dowmans Farm, just short of the farm buildings pass through a gate on the right and then turn left to reach the road. Turn left and follow the quiet road into the village. The infant River Churn is crossed, its water newly fresh from the limestone recesses of the Cotswolds.

From the river crossing continue with the road for a quarter of a mile until Coberley church is signed.

It is one of the stranger approaches to a church. The sign directs you through a small door of Coberley House to follow a path through a private garden to reach St. Giles' Church.

Coberley Hall once stood close by but only the churchyard walls remain to mark the one-time home of the famous Berkeley family. We have already encountered one of their descendants at Sudeley Castle, Sir John Bridges, who in the mid-sixteenth century became Lord Sudeley. The sundial, dated 1693, was the gift of another resident of the Hall, Paul Castleman, an improvement on the scratch dials that are found on the church walls.

Coberley has a connection with a favourite pantomime character, Dick Whittington. His home was at Pauntley, a few miles north west of Gloucester but he seems to have been a regular visitor to the Hall. The story depicts him as a young lad who made a vast fortune from humble beginnings. His cat, a champion rat and mouse-catcher, assisting him on his upward rise. This is all good stuff for the story teller. However it is doubtful that, when young Dick set off for London, he walked there with his lunch parcelled up in a red handkerchief dangling from the end of a stick.

Our hero was born about the middle of the fourteenth century, a son of the Lord of the Manor, and can safely be thought to have had a good start in life, despite a little problem his father had with those in authority. That he prospered through his own endeavours is not in doubt. 'Turn again Whittington' was indeed thrice Lord Mayor of London, was rich enough to be able to lend money to successive monarchs and yes, he did marry Alice Fitzwarren.

Richard's mother married twice, first Sir Thomas Berkeley, who contributed to Edward III's victory over the French at Crecy in 1346. Sir Thomas died in 1350 and he and his first wife, Joan, lie side by side in the church, in stony but comfortable repose. Sir Thomas is clad in knightly armour as befits his station and his wife in wimple and gown. The story does not stop here. Two years after the death of her first husband, Joan married Dick's father, Sir William Whittington. Sir William found himself in trouble with the crown and was outlawed. Some believe that this was because he failed to secure royal approval to his marriage into the powerful Berkeley family.

Another Berkeley is buried in the church, or to be more accurate, part of another Berkeley. Close to the altar, set into the wall, is the heart of Sir Giles Berkeley. He died away from his Coberley home, but the heart was brought back home for internment.

There is a strange story connected with Sir Giles. As you passed through the churchyard you may have noticed a tablet inscribed "Lombard 13thc." You may have supposed that this marks the last resting place of some local dignitary whose Christian name has unaccountably been omitted from the tablet. Not so, here in the hallowed ground has lain these six hundred and fifty years, a horse. Lombard by name and evidently Sir Giles' well-regarded, four-legged friend. It is possible that you might be in some difficulty if you presented yourself on your local vicar's doorstep and requested him to make the funeral arrangements for your horse. But then it would be quite a different matter if you were Lord of the Manor, member of an influential family, were probably responsible for the appointment of the incumbent and also bore the name of the church's patron saint.

After visiting the church, return to the road. Here turn left back towards the village. At a junction with a No Through Road, by a school sign, bear right and soon join the path signed to Seven Springs and Leckhampton Hill. Follow this good path for about 600 yards. When a narrow path appears on the right, take it, crossing a field between wire fences for 300 yards. On reaching the road, turn right to return to your starting point in 200 yards.

Walk 10: Leckhampton Hill

A shorter circuit to Devil's Chimney

Route: Daisy Bank Road – Devil's Chimney – Leckhampton Hill – Hartley Hill – Charlton Kings Common – Daisy Bank

Map: 1:50,000 Landranger Sheet 163, 1:25,000 Pathfinder 1089 (SO81/91)

Distance: 3½ miles

Parking: Car park at foot of Leckhampton Hill – Daisy Bank Road, which is found off the B4070 south of Cheltenham

This is a much shorter walk but Leckhampton Hill is such a splendid and enjoyable viewpoint that a second high/low circuit of the scarp is very worthwhile. The suggested route makes a good half day or evening walk, unencumbered by rucksacks that might be required for longer expeditions. It may also be useful to combine this with a visit to Crickley Hill, which is described in the next chapter.

If travelling south from Cheltenham, take the B4070 signed to Leckhampton and watch for Daisy Bank Road (easily missed) on the left. A small car park is found on the right – there is another space a little further on. The walk is described from the first car park.

Snakes Alive

You are welcomed with a warning "BEWARE OF ADDERS", an ominous caution quite properly issued by the Borough of Cheltenham Parks Dept. People do get bitten by snakes in this country and while this is likely to be an uncomfortable experience it is rarely fatal. Nevertheless medical attention should be sought immediately. Snakes do not welcome human intrusion and most times will make off without you being aware of their presence. As with the rest of the natural world, the advice is as always; watch, enjoy and do not disturb.

The Walk

From the first car park, take the path signed to Devil's Chimney, which rises steeply through the lower beech clad slopes of Leckhampton Hill. When the path opens out a little at the foot of an old quarry, bear right by the Leckhampton Hill Walk 3 sign. The path climbs again, and the trees fall back. A wide terrace is reached, with a sheer quarry face rising on your left, matched by a steep fall to the right. The Devil's Chimney soon comes into sight.

The views are superb, on a clear day, extensive and even when hazy, well worth the effort of the climb. There is also the consolation that this is the only upward pull of the walk. The immedi-

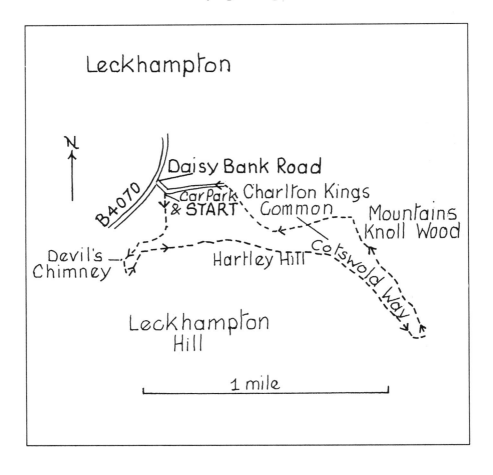

The Devil's Chimney, Leckhampton Hill

ate landscape has been refashioned by quarrying, with great bites take out of the hillside.

Quarrying in the Cotswolds

Cotswold stone is famous and has long been quarried for use both locally and further afield. The Painswick quarries are believed to date from Roman times. The most famous of all, at Taynton near Burford, are known to have been flourishing at the time of the Domesday survey of 1086. Stone from Taynton has found its way into many a historic building. It was sent by river to help build St. Paul's Cathedral. Oxford Colleges have called upon it for hundreds of years, as did the builders of St. George's Chapel and Windsor Castle.

Nearer at hand, the quarrymen of Leckhampton have been at work since medieval times, making full use of the thick layers of limestone, the depth of which is demonstrated at the Devil's Chimney. The transformation of Cheltenham to an important spa town, towards the end of the eighteenth century, was greatly helped by the ready supply of stone from which many of its buildings were constructed.

Cheltenham

In 1988, Cheltenham celebrated the two-hundredth anniversary of the extended visit to the town of George III and Queen Charlotte.

The fifty-year-old King was ill, and it had been thought that taking the waters at the then small spa town might help provide a cure. One suspects that the King's doctors were hard put to diagnose his complaint. To be seen doing something was better than doing nothing. It is now believed that he was suffering from porphyria, a disease, which upsets the body's metabolism and induces periods of insanity.

The town was amply rewarded for whatever benefit the king may have received from his five-week stay. Royal patronage transformed

Cheltenham into a fashionable resort ensuring rapid and continuing prosperity.

Cheltenham's story as a spa town had begun some seventy years earlier with the discovery by William Mason of a saline spring. Twenty years on, in 1738, Mason's son-in-law, Henry Skillicorn, built the first pump room. As the town started to grow so did the social activity, which was an important element in the life of the spas. By the seventeen eighties a theatre and assembly rooms had been built and a master of ceremonies recruited from the rival city of Bath.

Cheltenham was successful but not outstandingly so. Something more was needed to secure the patronage of the rich and powerful, and make a visit to Cheltenham an essential part of the social season, a place to see and to be seen. Fate took a hand and George III's unfortunate illness did the trick. A steady stream of the rich and powerful, and those with ambitions to be so, followed. The rest, as they say, is history.

Well known as the town is for its racecourse, parks, schools and cultural activities, there is a modern day addition, which has often been in the news. As the watcher on the Devil's Chimney looks down upon the towers and spires of the town, his eyes will be drawn to the large dish aerials of the Government Communications Head-quarters at the edge of the town. Here is Britain's listening post on the world. Giant ears cocked to the heavens, gathering and combing through in a sophisticated search of millions of items from the ether. Much of what is collected must be totally useless and an enormous sifting process goes on to uncover the little gold nuggets of informa-tion from a mountain of dross. Whatever may lie hidden beyond the high fences there is one secret, at the very least, which the Govern-ment cannot keep. For there is no disguising the huge dishes raised to the sky, sucking in the outpourings of a never silent world.

The Walk, continued

From the terrace above the Devil's Chimney, go forward for a short distance until a post on the left announces the Cotswold Way. Do not head south with it, but turn left and follow the waymarked route over the open summit and through the hill top camp. Thence onwards, through the remains of old quarries, to follow the edge of the scarp.

In addition to the abundance of wild flowers and butterflies, you are likely to see another native of Leckhampton Hill. This is the Roman Snail, the edible snail beloved by the French, which thrives in chalk and limestone country. It is our largest snail and, as its name suggests, it was not only the French that found it a culinary attraction.

After a while the path dips and follows a hollow way leading to a short wooded section. After leaving the trees turn right along the top edge of a field, then left down hill along its short edge. A rough track is followed for only a few yards to meet a crossroads of paths. At this point leave the Cotswold Way and take the left path through the trees.

After an intermittently muddy section the path emerges into the open to become a good dry track beneath the high scarp. There is a junction of paths at Mountains Knoll Wood. Take care not to be diverted northerly along the track to Sandy Lane but continue westerly over Charlton Kings Common. After the track widens and houses are met, continue forward on an improving road to return to your starting point.

Crickley Hill: viewpoint and archaeological site

Crickley Hill Country Park is found about four miles south of Cheltenham on the B4070. This airy viewpoint nudges into the Severn Vale, offering views across the border into Wales, to the long undulating line of the Malvern Hills, with Gloucester just a few miles to the west.

Whilst the Cotswold Way traverses the hill, I offer not a walk but a suggestion that a visit to this spot will provide more than a little gentle exercise.

Throughout our exploration of the Cotswold Way we have come upon ancient burial mounds and passed through hill top camps. It is from the excavation of these sites that archaeologists have been able to build up a picture of the way our forebears lived. An incomplete picture, a pale shadow rather than a full portrait, nevertheless a composition that is growing year by year as more is discovered and interpreted. We know little or nothing of their moral codes of conduct, their religious background, their family and tribal allegiances, how far it was a patriarchal or matriarchal society, whether sons were valued more than daughters. These questions require more than the uncovering of yesterday's artifacts to provide answers.

There is, of course, no written record. However, sharp stones, carved bones, broken pots, post holes, grains of cereal, arrow heads and pieces of jewellery make a contribution to an incomplete canvas, but one that is far from empty.

The Gloucestershire County Council has established an information centre at the park. It is being developed with audio visual displays detailing the history, geology, flora and fauna of Crickley Hill. This is not only a scheduled ancient monument, also a Site of Special Scientific Interest.

In addition to the facilities at the centre, leaflets illustrating self guided tours have been produced. These deal with man's occupancy of the hills during the Neolithic and Iron Age periods, the geology and ecology of the area.

The site has been under careful examination since 1969, with succeeding summers the scene of painstaking excavation. Over the years thousands of volunteer workers have spent most of July and August sifting the sands of prehistory to unravel the secrets of the past. Astonishingly, over a million items have been found, most of them very small indeed, but each a contribution to the mammoth jigsaw, which is slowly being pieced together. If you marvel that, in these days of hustle and rush, such patient uncovering and cataloguing can go on year after year, then you may like to make a point of visiting Crickley Hill open day. This is usually held annually on the first Saturday and Sunday in August.

Crickley Hill has been described as "the most important dig" in Europe, due to its occupation by differing communities over a long, but not continuous, period. If over twenty seasons of excavation seems a long time, and I understand that this represents about half the presently projected work, then it should be viewed against a calendar that extends back to 3500BC.

The work has revealed detail of stone, bronze and iron age settlements, as well as post-Roman occupation, up to around AD500. It is not the pieces of one jigsaw that are being collected, but several, and in combination with materials from more distant sites. Flint for example, one of stone age man's raw materials for domestic tools and weapons, is not found naturally locally. It was obtained from the Wiltshire Downs more than thirty miles away.

We toured the site watching the careful removal of the layers of soil, with trowel and brush. Slow work requiring great patience, picking over each foot of the ground with more attention than a barefooted man scrutinizes the floor after a major kitchen disaster.

As we watched something came to light. It proved to be an iron age ring. It was treated with great respect, direct contact with the excavators hands being studiously avoided because of the natural acids on the fingers. After logging, the ring transferred to tissue and then into a plastic bag.

Whatever conclusions the archaeologists come to from this particular find, it is certain that those spectators with a romantic and imaginative turn of mind had invented a story of their own to fit the ring. Whose finger had worn it, man, woman, or child? Was it crudely made in an idle moment or carefully crafted over long hours? Did it serve to seal a marriage, a token of undying love? Was it a symbol of authority, a child's plaything, a priest's badge of office, a precious gem, or a worthless bauble, a magic sign to ward off evil or a piece of vanity? Where lies the finger that wore it? How came it to be placed there, was it bartered, won in battle, stolen or lovingly given? However useless these last few lines of conjecture on the finger that wore the ring are, the open day does put some flesh on the bones of everyday living with demonstrations of various domestic crafts.

Digging into the past . . . open day on Crickley Hill

Workers on the site have learnt the tool-making and crafts of the people who would have lived on Crickley Hill. A flint knapper was at work and had made an arrow head. Flint, found in chalk areas, was a particularly useful resource. When the edge of a tool was lost the flint could be reknapped, and used on smaller tools or arrow heads as its size reduced. Hundreds of arrowheads have been uncovered on the site and the careful plotting of the positions in which they were found has helped to establish that the camp had come under attack on several occasions.

When the early farmers spread here from the continent, they brought seeds and livestock with them. A process of education began as the native inhabitants saw the benefits of organised farming and stock rearing. They resulted in higher standards of living than were obtainable from hunting and fishing activities.

Sheep were an important part of the economy. It had not only the virtue of feeding itself but in doing so its close grazing kept the re-emergence of scrub at bay after the forests were cleared. Sheep means wool and visitors were encouraged to try hand spinning and weaving on a crude loom. Pottery is an ancient art and a demonstration was in progress using clay brought up from the spring line. These early farmers produced cereal crops and the hand grinding of corn was another domestic chore to which the twentieth century visitor is introduced.

It all suggests a simple, hard working but not necessarily peaceful life. They would have had their fears as we do. They had a religion but whom they worshipped is a mystery. No doubt, they looked to some superior being to take care of them, to provide a good harvest, protection from their enemies, and the hope of a better life in the hereafter. Certainly the site had its special place set aside as a shrine, and it seems to have been in use for a long period, from around 2500BC. Something violent and dramatic happened to this temple. It was desecrated and destroyed, by whom and why we do not know. Did it produce a powerful magic that made its attackers fearful and so sought to bring it down? Did a generation lose their belief after a series of bad harvests or sickness? Did a rival tribe pull down their enemies' spiritual home to complete a physical conquest?

Today we may feel that we live in a modern civilisation, but in the long march of man we have moved only a little along the road from these hill-top dwellers. Like them we still eat the meat of cattle, pigs and sheep. Grain still provides our daily bread. Even the comfort of wool is prized above the convenience of synthetic fibre. We may live nearly three times as long, but our homes may still come under attack. We still celebrate the seasons and if the harvest comes more indirectly through the pay packet, we still look for its increase.

Those long gone people brought their children into the world, sang them to sleep in the cool of the evening and comforted them in the dark of the night. We still bow the knee to a superior being whether from convention or conviction. There are those who rarely take part in formal worship but do not dismiss the possibility that their time here on earth may only be part of a journey.

Yes, there is more to Crickley Hill than a pleasant stroll on a summer's afternoon.

Walk 11: Cheese Roll

Coopers Hill, Great Witcombe and the Roman Villa

Route: Birdlip – Great Witcombe – Roman Villa – Coopers Hill – High Brotheridge – Witcombe Wood – Birdlip

Map: 1:50,000 Landranger Sheet 163, 1:25,000 Pathfinder 1089 (SO 81/91)

Distance: 7 miles

Parking: Birdlip

Toilets: Close to route at Fidlers Elbow car park off A46

It should be noted that parts of this route can be uncomfortably muddy after heavy rain. Poor drainage and churning by horses may leave these sections like a glue pot. Boots are recommended.

The Walk

From Birdlip, follow the B4070 (south west) and after a short distance, take the path on the right signed to Coopers Hill and Prinknash Abbey. Follow the broad descending track through Witcombe Wood. After a while the Cotswold Way joins from the right via a deep hollow way and the familiar white-spot waymarking is seen. Note this is the junction for your return journey.

This is a cool path beneath tall beech trees along a steeply falling hillside. The nettle leaved bell-flower, a relative of the old garden favourite, the Canterbury Bell, may be seen. As with many of our wild flowers it boasts more than one name. Its aliases include Bats in the Belfry. I can see the bell-tower connection and assume bats is by association. More usefully it is also known as Throat-wort, a relic of its one time use for the relief of sore throats.

Gaps in the trees offer views to Coopers Hill as the descent steepens. In

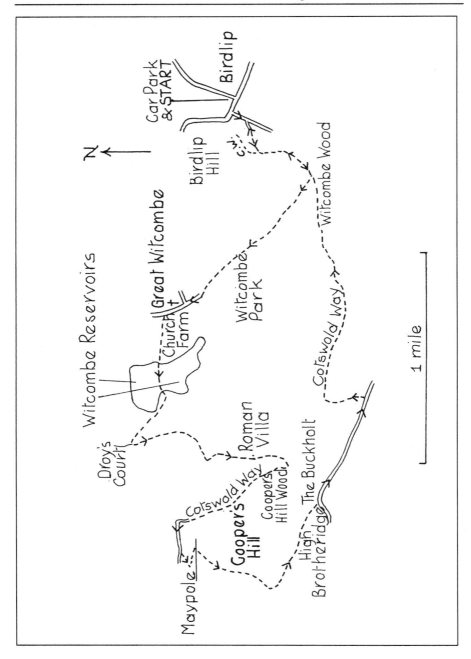

about a quarter of a mile, at a bend where some quarrying has taken place, leave the Cotswold Way. Take the path on the right, which ultimately leads to Great Witcombe. Turn right, downhill through woods passing a plantation of Norwegian spruce. As the trees fall back, the silver-grey gleam of the Witcombe reservoirs comes into sight, a foil to the wood crowned Coopers Hill. Watch for the path on the left, way-marked with a yellow arrow and a black spot. The path runs down into the valley with marker posts in the field. As you descend there is a distant glimpse of the tower of Gloucester Cathedral.

As the valley bottom is reached, pass through a gateway and turn right to follow the waymarked path for about a quarter of a mile to reach a metalled lane. Here turn right into Great Witcombe.

Great Witcombe

Great Witcombe is a tiny village, set in an amphitheatre of wooded hills of almost even height, Birdlip Hill, Coopers Hill and the scarred Crickley Hill. A little haven of peace and tranquillity, and long the home of the Hicks Beach family. The former school, school house and church nestle together. Very much the rural pattern of church and education set side by side with 'the big house', Witcombe Park, a little way off.

A giant yew, so often a feature of our country churchyards casts a great shadow over the gravestones and prompts the usual question how old? The adjective 'ancient' is obligatory in such circumstances, a cliche that can scarcely be avoided, although the church guide suggests a comparatively modest age of 250 years. Yew trees in churchyards are an old tradition. At day-school we were taught they were used to make bows and were planted within the confines of the churchyard since bark, berry and leaf were all poisonous and harmful to livestock. While at Sunday School it was suggested that the great spread of the tree's branches provided a ready meeting place before formal churches were built.

Another shadow falls upon the church, the sundial of 1751, made redundant, by a church clock installed just over a hundred years ago. In common with many old churches the walls have several scratch dials, otherwise known as mass clocks. The countryman worked by the sun, so should he also worship by the sun. However, one wonders why it was necessary for so many dials to appear upon the south wall of a single church. Were they replacements for dials that had grown less legible, or were they at times obscured by the shadows of churchyard trees, such as the yew. In this case the dials were, apparently, there long before the present tree. A little family competition might be a pleasant diversion – question how many scratch dials? The count appears to be six, one on the east wall and five on the south.

Within it is a truly rural church, still without electricity and with candle branches on many pews. There is an immediate impression of a great contrast between darkness and light. Dark on one side of the building, the light occluded by the stained glass windows. Bright on the other where the clear glass allows the daylight full reign.

There are memorials to various members of the Hicks Beach family. William 1841-1923, served the county in local administration and Parliament and was accorded the freedom of Cheltenham for his public services. Sir Percy Hicks Beach, was another Gloucestershire knight who fought at the battle of Crecy. Sir Michael Hicks Beach was an MP for 42 years (1864-1906) and twice Chancellor of the Exchequer. He acquired the nickname Black Michael, which sounds intriguingly villainous, more suited to a pirate than a respected politician and holder of various government offices.

After visiting the church, continue towards the village for 100 yards, then take the signed footpath on the left close to Church Farm. After a few steps the path turns right along a hedgerow. Towards the end of the field go through a kissing gate and forward as waymarked to the reservoirs. Take the causeway path to cross the reservoir then right along the waters edge to pass through an iron gate. Here, take the waymarked path over two fields to emerge onto a metalled lane, with Droys Court to your right.

Turn left and follow the lane for about three-quarters of a mile. There are good views to Great Witcombe, Witcombe Park, the tree-topped hill and the reservoirs.

Witcombe Roman Villa

When the car park for the Roman villa is reached, continue signed "To the monument." The small museum on the site is temporarily closed and the sign announcing this has the air of having been there for some time. However the ground-plan of the villa is there for all to see, even if the opportunity to inspect the mosaic, which is under cover, is lacking.

The villa covers an extensive area. The little spring, which can be heard as it falls out of the hillside, would have been an element in the choice of this site. Fresh clear running water for drinking and the all-important bath, and a commanding view of the land that was farmed, must have made it a very pleasant place in which to live and work. From the villa, can be seen, the scarred edges of Crickley Hill, the wooded circlet of the hills curving round Birdlip and the pattern of field and hedgerow running down to Witcombe. Close by is Coopers Hill Farm, successor to centuries of farming settlements on this spot.

From the villa return to the lane and turn left. The metalled road ends at the farm. Here go forward to a gateway into a field, then cross a stile to follow fence and hedge line on your right. After a short distance, pass through a further gateway, turning slightly to the right in the wood to follow a rising path. As the path levels out a little and starts to swing to the left, fish-hook right on a broad track along the wooded heights of Coopers Hill, once more with the Cotswold Way. This is mixed woodland with beech, ash and sycamore. After a while the path follows the edge of the wood, with a prospect of the spires of Cheltenham, the long whale backed Bredon Hill, the high plateau of Cleeve Hill. A wide panorama, enjoyed by the eye but not so easily captured by the camera. Many plants thrive on the woodland margins including wall lettuce, mullien, sun spurge and wound wort, another plant in the countryman's pharmacopoeia, reputed to have antiseptic properties.

A cottage is passed perched on the edge of the scarp, sheltered by the woods and with a view that must be worth a small fortune. The path works its way round the hillside and further houses come into view. The rough track becomes a narrow metalled lane as it leaves the Witcombe Estate.

The Haven, offers refreshments, bed and breakfast, and interesting conversation about this corner of the Cotswolds and the famous and jealously guarded Coopers Hill Cheese Rolling traditions. I am indebted to Rosemary Hellerman and to the Local History section of the Gloucester Central Library for some of the information that follows.

Cheese Rolling

At first sight, one thinks of this as another of those satisfying old village customs. Its origins, decently lost in the mists of time, with strong elements of pagan homage to the gods, whoever they maybe. Fertility rites, sun worship and the like may all be reasonably assumed, the shape of the cheese is itself suggestive of the sun. Despite the apparent prehistoric roots, it is also claimed to be an annual re-statement of a claim to common land rights. Quite how the cheese rolling was supposed to achieve this may seem a little strange. If you think of it as a demonstration of the right to be there, then it makes sense. The performance of an old ceremony, where the whole village joins in, meets the requirement very nicely.

It must be said at the outset that this is no gentle and polite custom kept on for old times sake and described by some as 'quaint'. It is a tough demanding scrambling breakneck race and the winner fully deserves the cheese with which he is rewarded. The truth of this will be amply demonstrated when you reach Coopers Hill and see the one-in-three hillside. Down here, competitors are sent helter-skelter to be caught at the finish line by members of the local rugby club strategically stationed to arrest their pell-mell progress.

A master of ceremonies, clad in a white smock coat and wearing flowers, with ribbons in his hat, is in charge of the proceedings. Four races are run, with an eight-pound cheese being sent rolling down the hillside hotly pursued by the hopeful contestants.

Each race is started by a different person, it being an honour to be invited to roll the cheese. There is something of what might be called a roll of honour amongst the competitors. One man has over the years won nineteen cheeses and, on one record breaking occasion, an eleven-year-old boy won three of the four cheeses on the same day.

Rosemary Hellerman has participated since childhood, both as a competitor and a 'cheese roller', and has compiled a scrap book of the event. The advance publicity for the year 1836 included on the bill of fare:

Two cheese to be run for.
One plain cake to be grinned for (grinning through a horse's collar)
One plain cake to be jumped in the bag for. (a sort of sack race?)
Horings (apples) to be dipped in the tub for.
Set of ribbons to be danced for,
Shimey (Chemise) to be run for.
Belt to be rosled (wrestled) for.
Bladder of snuff to be chattered for by old women.

Something for everybody, you might say.

Continue, on from the Haven, with the excellent views, which steadily improve. When a further group of houses is met, turn left by the post box and then bear right to gaze up the fearsome slope down which the cheese hunters hurtle. If you don't have the opportunity to see the event at first hand, you can at least get an impression of the lusty scene from a local pub sign, The Cheese Rollers on the A46 at Shurdington.

Follow the steeply rising path through the woods to the summit.

Crowning the hill is a lofty maypole topped by a cockerel, not the tallest in England, Welford on Avon has that honour. The maypole tradition is one that has survived as strongly as any, a relic of very old fertility rites at a season when spring is advancing into summer.

The view from the summit down the slope should quickly confirm that cheese rolling, Coopers Hill style, is not a challenge for the faint-hearted and that it is not only the cheese that has a bumpy journey. It is a fine prospect from the edge, the background painted with the now familiar outlines of the Malvern, Bredon and Cleeve Hills, and the towers and spires of those twin towns of Cheltenham and Gloucester below. A sight to be savoured before plunging back into the cover of the woods.

The Cheese Rollers inn sign

From the maypole, continue with the Cotswold Way, heading south on the well-signed path. After about half a mile the open ground of High Brotheridge is reached. Abandon the Cotswold Way and take the path on the left, with the woods to the left and open ground to the right. After a while the path deserts the immediate edge of the wood. Ignore the first north/south crossing and continue forward until some farm buildings are seen, about half a mile after leaving the Cotswold Way.

At this point turn right soon to meet a road. Here turn left and follow the road for half a mile until a path on the left is signed. Take this path northwards, waymarked by a yellow and green arrow, to rejoin the Cotswold Way after about a quarter of a mile. Take care not to take the left fork just before the Cotswold Way.

The junction with the Cotswold Way is a five-barred gate at the edge of the wood giving a nicely framed view of Witcombe and the hills. Turn right with The Way. This can be very muddy in places. When the Cotswold Way diverts left through a deep hollow way, remain on the upper track to return to the road, turn left for Birdlip and your starting point.

Should you miss the division of the paths, there is no need to turn back. Continue with the Cotswold Way as it drops downhill on a broad track. Eventually leave this, as the Cotswold Way fish-hooks right, following a narrow path through the trees, to reach the road a little below Birdlip. Here turn right, to return to the village.

Walk 12: The Fairway

Prinknash Abbey and Painswick Beacon

Route: Fidlers Elbow A46 — Prinknash — Kites Hill — Popes Wood — Painswick Beacon — Cranham Corner — Rough Park — Upton Wood

Map: 1:50,000 Landranger Sheet 162, 1:25,000 Pathfinder 1089 (SO81/91)

Distance: 5 miles

Parking: Coopers Hill Car Park, Fidlers Elbow A46

Toilets: Coopers Hill Car Park, Fidlers Elbow A46

This walk passes close to Prinknash Abbey but those wishing to visit may find it convenient to drive there first or call in at the end of the walk. (Details in Useful Information Section).

The Walk

The walk starts from the car park on the A46 a little over a quarter of a mile north east of the main entrance to the Abbey. From the car park cross the road and turn left along the busy A46, using the narrow path. After 400 yards, at a bend in the road, take the path on the right. Squeeze through the purpose-made gap in the wall, which assumes all walkers are on the slimmer side of large.

The main buildings of the Abbey are seen ahead, should you have no prior knowledge of this community then you are probably in for something of a surprise. Here there are no ancient cloisters to be seen where the faithful walk in silent contemplation. No lofty tower from which the sonorous chiming of a bell calls the monks to the offices of the day. No great arches or other familiar signs of ecclesiastical architecture to proclaim its dedication to matters spiritual in a temporal world. On the contrary, from this distance you might assume that you are looking at a modern school or the administrative headquarters of some commercial organisation, which had wisely decided to move to the countryside for the sake of its employees' health and corporate wealth. Closer acquaintance will permit some revision of these impressions.

Cross a short, nettle-filled field. Then go through a metal gate and over a further field along a path which runs close to a wire fence. At the foot of the field, pass over a stile and maintain your forward direction to the stile seen at the bottom of the field. Here there is a waymark, forward, with a large chestnut tree immediately ahead, almost barring the way. The path leads to the edge of a coppice at the valley bottom, with the path waymarked forward. At the bottom of the field cross a stile and then a footbridge over a small stream to go forward to meet and cross a track. Take the rising path, which follows the edge of the field with the fence to your left. Part way up the field the path makes a little wriggle to cross into and follow the margin of the next field. The path meets the road, close to a cottage where figs are to be seen growing on the wall.

Turn left to follow this quiet lane for about a quarter of a mile. Just after passing the gateway of a house called Kites Hill, take the bridleway on

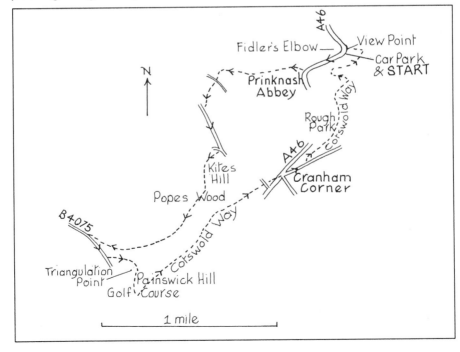

the right (the sign is almost hidden in the trees) to enter Popes Wood, a nature reserve. This ancient beech wood is under the management of English Nature but the public are permitted to walk on any of the tracks. A map showing these is situated at several entry points to the wood.

The path rises for a short distance before entering a small clearing with three paths. Take the central bridleway waymarked with a blue arrow and follow this until the road is reached in about one mile. Ignore all left and right turns. When the path edges the wood, Gloucester can be seen to the right but a far wider view will soon be on offer. Buzzards may be seen, they have bred successfully in the Painswick Hill area in recent years, and badger setts may also be noticed.

The road is reached, by a bus stop. Turn left, signed to Painswick. In a quarter of a mile, at a bend in the road, take the rising track on the left. This works its way round the slopes of Painswick Hill. There are a number of wild flowers to be seen along the banks, harebells, orchids, scabious, knapweed and yellow hawkweed. The path levels out to emerge into the open, by a war time pill box at the edge of a golf course. Here turn right on the crossing path and make your way towards the summit triangulation point.

Painswick Beacon

Here is another fine Cotswold viewpoint. As you walk round the ramparts of the old fort you may feel you are at the hub of the visible world. A circle with a rim bounded by countless hills. There is May Hill with its distinctive clump of trees. The sun burns away the mists of the morning to reveal Gloucester and its cathedral, and the silvery gleam of the widening River Severn. Bredon Hill, like May Hill, so often in the walker's eye, adds a touch of familiarity to the scene. Away to the south, the Tyndale Monument set high on Nibley Knoll points a symbolic finger to the heavens.

Closer at hand are the former quarries, from which the white limestone came to build Painswick. The Romans, nicely settled in Gloucester, drew upon its resources as did the builders of the cathedral. In 1988 the four-hundredth anniversary of the defeat of the Spanish Armada was celebrated here with the traditional

View from Painswick Hill Fort

bonfire. These celebrations captured the imagination of the British people. Thousands turned out to climb to beacon-hills the length and breadth of the land to watch for the distant, 'twinkling points of fire' that once raised the alarm, and to cheer on the spreading of the word as their local hill top burst forth with its fiery message. The efficacy of this method of communication was proven beyond doubt. Little more than half an hour passed from the setting of the first flame in the southwest, to the alarm being raised in the north. Strangely a golf course has one of its greens within the circle of the hill-fort. An American golfer, more concerned with the landscape than his game, confided to me that on a clear day this was one of the finest views he knew. That is quite a compliment from a native of a country with a superlative landscape of its own.

To resume the walk, make your way down from the fort to join the Cotswold Way. This can be seen running over the golf course, on a roughly NE-SW line, about 300 yards from the triangulation point. Turn left along The Way, which is now followed for most of the rest of this walk.

Follow the waymarked path over the golf course to join a broad track that leads to a metalled road running along the edge of Popes Wood. After 200 yards or so, as the road bends to the right, leave it and go forward on a broad track through Buckholt Wood, another part of the nature reserve. In a quarter of a mile meet and cross a small road, and continue through the wood. After 200 yards the path emerges on to the A46, which is crossed to take the road signed to Cranham and Birdlip.

The Cotswold Way soon leaves the road to take a woodland path on the left. This is a rising and falling route, which is followed for about a mile with occasional glimpses of Prinknash Abbey through the trees.

Prinknash Abbey

The Benedictine community came to the Cotswolds in the late 1920s, moving from their former island home on Caldey off the Pembrokeshire coast. Although this uprooting took place some seventy years ago the monks have yet to complete the Abbey church to bring their work to its fulfilment. Until the time is ripe to enter upon such an important and lasting building their worship takes place in the crypt.

This church, which is open to visitors, is of great interest and you may wonder if its design is a precursor of what will be seen when the Abbey church is built. The windows, in modern style, glazed in a multitude of colours, bring in kaleidoscopic pools of light to brighten the dimness. A dimness that is in no way suggestive of gloom, more of a careful control of the light value, just as the quieter passages of a great symphony provide the more peaceful moments.

The move from Caldey must have created many logistical problems, not the least the bells they brought with them. Being without a tower for their peal of eight, the bells remain outside, hung, not high above the monastery, but in an open frame at ground level. You may see one of the monks walk across the lawn to strike the bells. What a jubilant peal will ring out when the bells are finally hoisted into the belfry to celebrate the completion of the venture started, in 1928, when the monks left their storm-swept island for the green crowned hills of the Cotswolds.

The monastery is a farming and an artistic community. You have passed through their fields and, in the church, will have seen some of the work of the brothers. Prinknash Pottery is well known with its characteristic pewter colour. The skill and mystique in the operation of the potter's wheel may be watched from the viewing gallery. A bird park provides a colourful diversion for the family visitor.

On the hillside beyond the monastery gardens, is St. Peter's Grange, the Retreat House of the Abbey. The manor house, with its chapel, was once in the ownership of Gloucester Abbey. It is fitting that after a long, secular history it has returned to the hands of the church.

Ignore the crossing paths at a triangular meeting of ways and continue on the Cotswold Way. After a short distance leave it and descend by the steps on the left to return to your starting point. Before leaving the woods, take the signed diversion to the viewpoint. This includes such diverse features as the bright tower of Gloucester Cathedral with the competing splash of white on the nearby hillside that marks an artificial ski slope, the ancient Forest of Dean beyond the Severn and the airfield from which the famous Gloucester Gladiator first flew.

The Fair Lady: Exploring Painswick

Painswick is an elegant lady. Her skirts sweep down to the valley floor where the little stream makes a hem to her dress. Her head is held high, symbolised by the church spire that reaches out to touch the sky. Her clothes do not have the vulgarity of the latest fad but the enduring quality of garments skilfully tailored from the finest materials and worn with dignity and style.

Here is a lady who has long been accustomed to prosperity. The poor do not age well, but Painswick is growing old gracefully. Maturity sits well upon her and she is aglow with good health. Not that she has always had a peaceful life. Men at arms have advanced in good order across her hills, marching in time to the insistent beat of the drum, with the cheerful mixture of hope and fear of soldiers who have not yet been engaged in the bloody reality of war. The defeated and disillusioned have trodden the same hills, in less good order, heavy of heart and step, tired and hungry. Those not too numbed by their experiences reflecting whether perhaps there might be a better way to resolve conflict than by clash of arms, when all too often there are no winners. How often do the victors share that thought?

Painswick's history is long and that which has been recorded in the official guide to the village often touches upon the great names that have appeared in the wider chronicles of this country. Its pages are filled with two thousand years of incident and interest. If ever Painswick residents set out to produce a pageant, they will have no shortage of material on which to build a colourful production.

Those who come to visit this little jewel of the Cotswolds will naturally start their tour of the village with the parish church of St. Mary's. It is famed beyond the bounds of Gloucestershire with its wealth of churches. It is among the most handsome and a leading contender for the title (if there is one) of the best kept churchyard.

Overseas visitors to this country must find themselves overwhelmed by the panoply of history that is paraded before them. The stately homes of the great and powerful; the craftsmanship of artists and masons enshrined within the centuries-old cathedrals; parklands and gardens created by landscape architects; palaces of kings and the haunting of draughty corridors; mysterious stone circles; stories of the sieges of great castles; and strange country customs. Much of this kaleidoscope of craft, culture and conflict must quickly dissolve into a great sea of blurred impressions with one or two islands rising above the confused, swirling waters of memory. Painswick church must surely be one that is well remembered.

Painswick is a place of great character, built with the near white limestone from local quarries, which the Romans had been pleased to use when they settled in Glevum (Gloucester). The interest is centred on the church but the village should not be neglected for it is a place at one with itself.

"Proud Painswick" they say, which seems an all-too-convenient alliteration but the visitor quickly senses that pride. A better word might be love, which is demonstrated by the parishioners on duty in St. Mary's, eager to show its treasures to the steady stream that passes through its doors during the summer months.

The churchyard is perhaps more famous than the church itself and for more than one reason. It is best known for its shaped yew trees. The legend is that there were ninety-nine trees and attempts to extend their number to a nice, round hundred were always thwarted by the failure of the century tree to grow. The yews are now just over two hundred years old and in fine health. So they should be, for these long-lived trees have received much care and attention. The National Trust has described them as "of national importance" and compared them with the topiaried gardens at Levens Hall and the famous Sermon on the Mount at Packwood. This places them in very distinguished company and the church authorities have been careful to take expert advice in the conduct of their maintenance programme. Yews are slow growers, about an inch a year, but this does not mean they can be left alone with a casual clip now and again when they begin to look untidy. Each year the trees are inspected. Damaged ones have their tops removed to encourage growth and the trees are reshaped. Here they stand in the well-ordered manner of a regiment on parade, shoulder to shoulder, not a twig out of place, some making a guard of honour along the paved paths that crisscross the neat lawns of the churchyard, others linked together to provide triumphal arches through which the visitor may pass on his tour of inspection.

There is more to see here than the carefully manicured trees. The handsome lych gate was built at the beginning of the twentieth century using timber from the belfry when the old bell frames were discarded. Carved bells run up the gable end of the gateway, a thoughtful remembrance but then almost everything hereabouts is done with care.

Yews apart, the churchyard is famed for its remarkable collection of tombs dating from sixteen hundred onwards. They are the work of local masons, commemorating the mercers, clothiers, wool staplers and millers of the village. Clear evidence of the prosperous harvest reaped from the sheep's back. Other trades and crafts particularly mentioned include the butcher, baker and candlemaker of the old rhyme. I am not sure how far we can progress with that old skipping song, Tinker, Tailor, Soldier, Sailor, Rich man, Poor man, Beggar man, Thief. The tailoring connection is clearly represented. A soldier, he died in an Egyptian campaign in the Napoleonic Wars. There is not shortage of rich men, but I looked in vain for the other connections. The wrongdoer is not forgotten. His memorial, if such it is, can be found beyond the churchyard wall, the unusual spectacle-like, iron stocks. The tombs are of such interest and importance that two Tomb Trail leaflets have been produced to help visitors on a self guided tour of the churchyard. Its tributes to the departed manifested in many shapes and sizes, triangular, table-topped and round tombs.

The church was treated with scant reverence during the Civil War as the pock marks of cannon shot on the tower bear witness without and literary relics within. It is a handsome tower, topped by an equally fine spire, a landmark for miles. The walker exploring the surrounding hills will pick out its graceful stone needle from all

Lych gate of Painswick Church

points of the compass. Whist those closer at hand will admire its brightly painted clock face.

The spire of 1632 also suffered damage, not at the hand of man but by the no-less-violent forces of nature. A lightning strike brought the top tumbling down, but not wasted, it now stands close to the pulpit, a unique flower stand.

The ancient custom of 'Clipping the church' is still perpetuated each September. In today's language this is at first sight confusing, since clipping is not a barber-like trim, but an encircling of the church by the children of the parish who join hands to sing and dance. It's an old ceremony that was revived about a hundred years ago. Its origins are obscure, but the unbroken circle is full of symbolism, and speculation that it has pagan roots may not be too far wrong. After the ceremony, children are rewarded for their efforts with a bun and a silver coin.

While on the subject of local customs, a mention must be made of Puppy Dog Pie, also associated with this time of the year. The pie crust is supported in the usual way by a china dog. However, we are asked to believe that it originated when a local landlord found his cupboard empty of provisions and was obliged to slaughter his dog to provide the necessary filling for the meat pie ordered by his patrons. It may be a good story, but is a delicacy that is only likely to whet the appetite in times of desperate starvation. For pet lovers, it is too painful to contemplate.

Britain is the home of change ringing, a long tradition that served to call people to worship, to ring out in joyful celebration in times of victory, or, half muffled, to pay their last respects to the dead. Most village churches can only aspire to, at most, a peal of eight bells. Painswick has a cathedral-like twelve. They are justly proud of their bells and campanologists on tour are happy to accept an invitation to St. Mary's belfry. The local band of ringers have a title as splendid as, and indeed older than, some of their bells. They are the Ancient Society of Painswick Youths, founded in 1686.

The bells were cast between 1686 and 1821, with some of the earlier bells recast in 1731. Bells invariably carry an inscription, often the date and the names of the church wardens or the incumbent. Painswick's inscriptions include "Prosperity to this town and parish" and "I to the church the living call and to the grave do summon all."

Two memorials may be mentioned, one from the twentieth century, the other much older. The first is to a man of great distinction, "Willoughby Hyett, Baron Dickinson of Painswick, P.C., K.B.E. . . . Founder and Leader of the first British Society advocating the formation of a League of Nations and the World Alliance for promoting Peace through the churches. . ." The second memorial, a tomb in St. Peter's Chapel has a strange history insofar as it has accommodated three unrelated families. The earliest dates back to 1356, Viscount Lisle, later in 1540, no less a person than the Governor of the Tower of London, Sir William Kingston. The effigies now seen on the tomb are those of a seventeenth century Chancellor of Gloucester, Dr. Seaman and his wife. It seems likely that this learned man and his good lady are here to stay and will not suffer the disturbance of their predecessors.

The storm clouds of the Civil War passed this way and the nearby Court House did temporary duty as the Royalist centre of operations. In 1643, Gloucester with its Parliamentary garrison was under siege for some time, until the King's men found it prudent to withdraw when news of a relief force reached them. Early in the following year there was further activity in the Painswick area with the ground passing from one side to the other. The village was recaptured from the Parliamentarians in March but not before some considerable damage had been done to the church both by fire and cannon shot.

A soldier of the Parliamentarian army, evidently a man of letters, left his mark in the north aisle while imprisoned there at one stage of the Civil War. No doubt the adapted quotation from Edmund Spenser's Faerie Queene, "Be bold, be bold, but not too bold," reflected his thinking at the time. As the King's cause was being lost, one of his men might well have drawn upon a quotation from the same author, " . . . all for love and nothing for reward."

It is all too easy when popping in and out of churches on a walking tour to think of them as little more than museums. It is an attitude of mind that is, to some extent, encouraged. They are so often the valued home of the work of skilled craftsmen and artists, inevitably closely bound up with the history of the area and sometimes with that of the nation. That they are for the most part in such good order today is a tribute to the faithful, who having inherited the legacy of their parish church, have recognised that they are trustees for a time. They have a duty of care so that it may be passed on to the next generation for the purpose that the original builders intended. Painswick has clearly accepted the challenge. The whole place shines with the polish of tender loving care. An addition made to the church in the past few years serves to illustrate the point. A collection of over three hundred embroidered kneelers has been assembled. They represent the life of church and village, its history and its present activities. Flora and fauna are depicted, as are the badges of many organisations both civil and military. To go further would be to risk degenerating into a catalogue but three may be mentioned; a local meals on wheels delivery, a particularly attractive aerial view of the church with its famous yew trees and one commemorating the Ramblers Association's half century.

A walk around the village is a pleasant experience. Drop down to the valley bottom where four of the score or more mills that drew power from the stream still remain, albeit as private residences. Pop into the post office, dating from 1400, the oldest building in use as a post office. Gaze into the windows of Drumbeat, "Toy soldier makers to the world." Keep a look out for the donkey doors, which allowed passage to that ancient beast of burden, or browse in the Little Fleece Bookshop. If time permits, walk the quiet lanes to the surrounding hamlets and enjoy the view of Painswick from further afield, which is just what is planned in the next chapter.

Walk 13: The King with no Home

Haresfield Beacon circuit

Route: Painswick Valley — Sheephouse — Wades Mill — Pitchcombe — Harefield Farm — Standish Wood — Haresfield Beacon — Cliff Well — Scottsquar Hill — Washbrook — Painswick

Map: 1:50,000 Landranger Sheet 162, 1:25,000 Pathfinder 1113 (SO 80/90)

Distance: 9 miles

Parking: Stamages Lane, Painswick (off the A46 on the Stroud side of the village)

Toilets: Stamages Lane, Painswick (off the A46 on the Stroud side of the village)

The Walk

The walk starts from the car park at the top of Stamages Lane. The lane falls steeply to the valley. After crossing Kingsmill Lane, it becomes Stepping Stones Lane and continues to the Painswick stream.

This little brook provided the power to turn the mills, which, with the large flocks of sheep grazing the hills, were the foundation of Painswick's prosperity. The industry moved away from the village as more power was needed for the increased production made possible by improved methods. The nearby Stroud Valley was famous for its West of England Cloth. Output increased to such an extent that the Cotswold flocks were unable to keep up with the demand and additional supplies had to be purchased from Europe and later from Australia. Nothing lasts for ever, the busy looms of Stroud, Stonehouse, Nailsworth and other Gloucestershire mill villages gradually fell silent, victims of competition and the slowing demand for the fine cloth in which they were the acknowledged specialists, as cheaper products were favoured. By the beginning of the twentieth century the industry was a pale shadow of its former self.

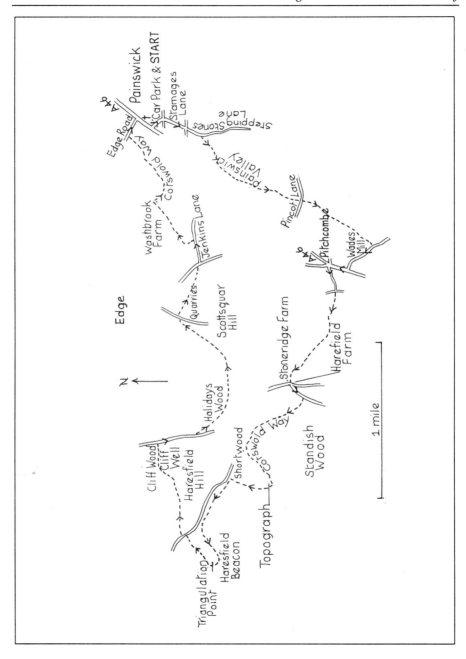

Four of Painswick's mills survive today, not as working mills but converted to domestic residences; Loveday's Mill, Savory's Mill, Cap Mill and Painswick Mill. Savory's can claim the honour of being last man out, surviving the decline in the area by adapting to the changing circumstances. It swapped from cloth production to the grinding of corn and later to the manufacture of hairpins and similar items. Locally it is referred to as the Pin Mill. Cap Mill of course speaks for itself. The mills are not on the route of this walk but a short stroll along Kingsmill Lane and the footpath at the valley bottom will provide a glimpse of them today in their new role.

Cross the stream. Ignore the first path that runs along the bank and take the next path on the right (a wide metalled track with good views back to the village). This is followed for nearly half a mile to Sheephouse. The track then disappears but continue forward to pass between the buildings with Dove Cote Cottage on your right. After a short distance pass through a gateway, with the path yellow waymarked, and maintain your direction over the fields heading for Pincott Lane. The path is not always distinct as it crosses rough pasture but the waymarking will keep you on the right route. The path dips down between trees to cross a stream by a plank bridge. It then rises and goes slightly to the right to pick up a waymarked path at the field corner. Go ahead to reach Pincott Lane by Wick Street and Primrose Cottages.

Cross the lane and take the path between the two cottages. The waymarked, but not always clear on the ground, route runs southwesterly. After a quarter of a mile, it runs close to the field boundaries on your left to reach Wades Lane in a further quarter of a mile. Turn right, down the narrow lane, edged with black bryony, hops, brambles and burdock. After about 400 yards cross the Painswick Stream. Wade Mill is on the right.

Beyond the mill the lane rises to meet the A46, here turn right and at a junction take the lane on the left signed to Pitchcombe. After about 300 yards, when a crossing road is met, continue forward on the No Through Road. As forecast, the metalled road soon ends. Take the path beyond a gate and head uphill towards a wood. Looking back over the valley the handsome house on the hillside is Brownshill Court.

On reaching the woods, go forward through a gate and head uphill. The path edges diagonally left across a field to reach the wood's edge. Follow its outside edge (on your left). At the top of the field, pass over the waymarked stile by a metal gate. Follow through to meet a road, with Harefield Farm on your left and Stoneridge Farm to your right.

Turn left with the road for a few yards, then take the lane on the right signed to Randwick, which is followed for about 100 yards. Ignore the first footpath signed outside the wood and continue a few more yards to enter the National Trust's Standish Wood.

Take the waymarked path that passes through a narrow gap and curves into the wood. After 200 yards it meets a broader path, turn right on this. The Cotswold Way has now been joined and is followed back to Painswick.

Continue through the wood and shortly after a gateway a cleared space is met, with a seat well-placed for you to pause and enjoy the view.

This spot is at the centre of a horseshoe scooped out of the hills. The wooded ridge to the left and the partly cleared hillside to the right make the points of the shoe. Ahead the woods fall off to the valley, below is Standish Park Farm and beyond, the gleam of the broadening River Severn on its twisting course through the vale. Sheep graze the hillside with cattle in the lower fields. The tall white chimneys at the edge of Stonehouse identify the creamery. The long established activities of the countryside contrasting with the twin tower blocks of the Berkeley Nuclear Power Station.

Continue through the wood until the Shortwood car park is reached. Take the path to the edge of the scarp and the topograph view point

The topograph, placed here in 1934, is laid out as a relief map. Over the years it has acquired a patina pleasant to the touch. The detail of the roads, streams and valleys, together with the indicators of more distant points, are still clear. We are promised, weather conditions being favourable, views to May Hill 11½ miles, the Black Mountains 40 miles, the Sugar Loaf 35 miles, the Brecon Beacons 51½ miles, Dunkery Beacon 71 miles, Steep Holme in the Bristol Channel 48 miles and the Tyndale Monument 9½ miles. Really clear days are at a premium and the oncoming clouds over the Forest of Dean may well leave many of these promises unfulfilled. This is not the only high point of the walk and there will be another opportunity to scan the horizon and wonder whether that distant smudge is the Welsh mountains reaching up to the clouds or the clouds bearing down to cloak them in invisibility.

The path from the car park to the topograph is one leg of a 'V'. To continue, take the other leg, as waymarked on the topograph, over the pasture with St. John's wort and harebells flourishing with some handsome woolly thistles. When the road is almost reached, the path swings left falling by way of Bunkers Bank. Shortly after passing through a gateway, the path rises half right. At the top of the steeply-stepped climb to the road edge, turn left along the path passing the National Trust's Haresfield Beacon sign. The path winds round the old hill fort to reach the triangulation point.

On this windy hilltop there are views across the Severn to the Forest of Dean, the flat plain of the Vale, with its patterned fields.

Haresfield Beacon

Much of it is down to pasture, as befits a famous cheese making county. The rural activity is broken by the M5, busy with dinky cars and lorries, with a model train running along the railway line to Gloucester. The cattle in the fields confirm the impression of a child's toy village. The old aerodrome at Moreton Valence from which the fighters once flew is now a trading estate, a modern version of beating swords into plough shares.

To resume, take your direction from the faint waymark on the triangulation point, i.e. right. A stile is soon reached. The path follows the scarp edge of Ring Hill, to descend to the road about a quarter of a mile from the trig point. Turn left and in a short distance take the Cotswold Way on the right, signed to Painswick, found opposite Ringhill Farm. A broad track is followed under Haresfield Hill. Along the way, set in the dark gloom cast by a yew tree, will be found a stone. It's none too easy to read the inscription, which records the end of the siege of Gloucester on the 5th September, 1643.

The Siege of Gloucester

This stone with its fading inscription commemorates an event of the dark days of the Civil War. Charles I had quarrelled with his Parliament, a clash that led to armed conflict. That most tragic of wars, Civil War, spread across the land, making enemies of friends, bringing down great men and great houses, destroying men and the crops they had planted.

Much of the war was fought in the Midlands. In its towns and villages you will find the marks of the conflict on church walls, tales of local skirmishes that never found their way into the books recording the big set-piece battles. The events of the summer of 1643 in this place have all the elements of high drama, of the waiting game of the siege, of a city cut off and about to be overwhelmed. It happened like this:

The summer campaign was well under way. The Royalists had achieved some successes and by August the war had reached a point of balance, where victory might have been within their grasp . . . if only the right military decisions had been made.

The Royalist army had advanced on Gloucester, hoping for its early surrender. It was not to be and the siege that started on the

10th August had still not achieved its purpose when the calendar moved to the next month. Inside the walls of the city the defenders could not be feeling anything but deserted and desperate as supplies dwindled away. By the 5th September they were down to their last three barrels of gunpowder – but the Royalists did not know that. What the beleaguered Parliamentarians didn't know was that help was on the way, a large force on the march from London was close at hand. The Royalists could not face the prospect of a major battle. They withdrew and, by the 8th September, the Earl of Essex and his army marched into the city to scenes of rejoicing that may be imagined.

There is a poignant story told about the Gloucester campaign. The details vary but in essence during the retreat through Painswick, the King was asked by his son, "Father, when can we go home?" Charles is said to have replied, "We have no home to go to." A little cameo, true or not, from which the last drops of pathos may be wrung. Not that all was lost at that stage but . . .

Continue through the woods until a stepped path leads down to the road by Cliff Well.

For safety's sake, the top of the well has been concreted over but the winch remains, as does the inscription dating from 1870.

Deo Gratius
Who E'ere The Bucket Fall Upwindeth
Let Him Bless God Who Water Findeth
Yet Water Here But Small Availeth
Go Seek The Well That Never Faileth

At the lane, turn right. Ignore the first path on the left through Tump Farm. About 300 yards after leaving the well, take the bridleway on the left signed to Painswick, which runs through Hallidays Wood. Here there are tall beeches, ash and sycamore, a familiar pattern of these wooded hillsides. The way passes on through the National Trust's Stockend Wood.

Again you may see evidence of badger occupation. A sett with several entrances is clearly still in use, with signs of their tracks down the hillside where dead leaves have been pulled onto the path.

The path gives way to a broader track by a house. After 200 yards, the Cotswold Way is signed off right on a narrow path. It makes a winding progress uphill to reach a road by the old quarries of Scottsquar Hill. Cross the road and descend into the quarry watching out for the Cotswold Way sign ahead.

From the quarry top there are excellent views towards Painswick with its ubiquitous church spire. Follow the descending waymarked path with its prospect of the village and the hills. There are wild flowers in abundance. Keep an eye open for the marker posts, which guide you downhill to a join a narrow, high-banked hollow way. Reach the road, at the edge of Edge, just short of Edgemoor Inn.

Turn right with the road and in a short distance turn left on Jenkins Lane, which is followed for 300 yards. Just before a farm is met, take the path on the left signed to Edge and Painswick, passing through a narrow gap in a dry stone wall. Go forward for 100 yards then right over a waymarked stile. The path descends to the bottom-right of the field. Follow a stepped path through trees to cross a small stream by a footbridge. Continue through trees and then fields to reach Washbrook Farm, here turn right. The farm carries the date 1691 and the initials HWA.

From the farm your direction is indicated by the Painswick steeple. Take the waymarked path uphill passing attractive houses and gardens to reach the road. Turn right on Edge Road to arrive at Painswick church by the lych gate. Turn right to return to the Stamages Lane car park.

Walk 14: Bury and Barrow

Uley Bury hill fort

Route: Frocester Hill — Nympsfield — Uley — Uley Bury — Peaked Down (edge) — Cam Long Down — Coaley Wood — Frocester Hill

Map: 1:50,000 Landranger Sheet 162, 1:25,000 Pathfinder 1132 (ST69/79) and parts of three others!

Distance: 8 miles

Parking: Coaley Peak Picnic Site at Frocester Hill B4066

Toilets: Coaley Peak Picnic Site at Frocester Hill B4066

The walk starts from the picnic site about five miles south west of Stroud. I have not given full details of the 1:25,000 maps since the walk is inconveniently spread across four sheets. However, the greater part will be found on Pathfinder 1132.

Coaley Peak offers excellent views to the west, a topograph, information board, toilets and has the Nympsfield long barrow within its boundaries. The barrow, dated about 2500BC has been the subject of several excavations with the stonework of the roofless passages left open to view. More exciting is Hetty Pegler's Tump, another long barrow whose intriguing name derives from a seventeenth century landowner. It is a little off the route of the walk but worth a visit for the mild adventure of diving into the darkness of its burial chambers. The tump is about a mile further south. To gain admittance, it may be necessary to obtain the key from a cottage on the right-hand side of the road about half a mile nearer to Uley. A torch is necessary, the ability to stoop low and remain in that position is essential and your best suit should be left at home in the wardrobe. Photographers will need a flash gun. Items found in various excavations include human skeletons and boars' tusks.

The Walk

Leave the car park and turn right on the road to take the path on the left that crosses fields to the edge of Nympsfield. Turn left at the road and soon right, signed to Nympsfield village. The village pub, the Rose and Crown, seems to have set out to win a Britain in Bloom competition with window boxes, tubs and hanging baskets at every available place. Take the right fork at this point passing the Malt House, ignore the footpath on the right and continue to the church.

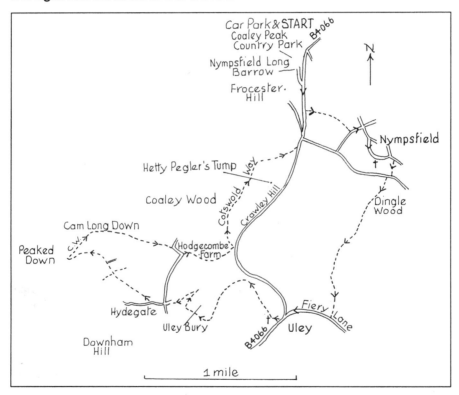

St. Bartholomew's Church, successor to a chapel first founded here in 1020, is a cool retreat. Its first recorded vicar was Adam the clerk in 1185. The present building dating from 1861, was built at a cost of £3,000 to replace the twelfth century church, but retains a late fifteenth century tower.

The Rose and Crown at Nympsfield

There is an old rhyme associated with the village, a copy of which will be seen on the church wall.

> "Nympsfield is a pretty place
> Built upon a tump
> And what the people live upon
> Is Heg Peg Dump."

Heg Peg Dump, it must be explained, is a pudding filled with fruit gathered from the hedgerows.

From the church turn right, downhill and shortly after the junction with another lane, take the signposted path on the right near some pretty cottages. The path climbs a steep bank then over a field to meet and cross a road to take the waymarked path opposite. At the bottom right-hand corner of the field, cross a stile by a metal gate and turn left.

In a short distance cross a further stile into Dingle Wood and go forward on a descending path. At the wood's edge, continue along a waymarked path with woods to the left and right. Skirt a large mound on your right soon to join a farm track heading south. The track is pursued through open ground, with Owlpen Wood to your left, to reach Fiery Lane in about three-quarters of a mile. Turn right to Uley village.

Uley, at one time taking a share in the general prosperity of the weaving trade, is a delightful place. It is set beneath wooded hills, a million miles away from the frantic activities of financial markets and the clangour of industry.

Our route passes close to St. Giles' church. Within, the record of benefactors includes a Mr Parslow, who left ten shillings per annum to give bread to the poor on St. John's Day. Henry Pegler (he of Hetty Pegler's Tump fame), who died in 1695, gave "ten shillings per annum to be paid out of Broadstone field in Uley, five shillings to be given away in bread to the poor and five shillings to the minister for a sermon to be preached on the 17th day of February."

From the church, take the path signed to Uley Bury, which follows the churchyard wall and the handsome Wellingtonian tree overtopping the church tower. On reaching a private car park area by a wooden garage go forward to a gate and into a field before turning right uphill towards the wood. It is a steepish climb with improving views.

A gate leads into the wood to the right of a little spur of trees. Take the rising path roughly north west. As the trees thin, a stile is seen and crossed to reach the south east corner of Uley Bury.

Uley Bury

Because of its superb location, walkers may find this the most interesting of the hillforts encountered so far. The long and steep approaches ensuring that an attacker would be breathless and in less than good order, forced into an assault in difficult circumstances. It is a rectangular site, about half a mile wide with a path following the perimeter, the centre being under cultivation.

On arriving at the summit turn left to follow the ramparts to the southern corner.

As the trees fall back, the views are superb. You are at eye level with the long ribbon of trees that garland the heights across the valley. To the southwest is the tall tower of the Tyndale monument above North Nibley. Below are the roof tops of Uley with the prominent church tower.

Turn right along the short edge of the camp to enjoy the beautifully shaped Downham Hill with its single line of trees on the summit. From the next corner the view is to the River Severn and the towers of the Berkeley Nuclear Power Station; to the north west is the high ground of Cam Long Down to which we are now heading.

From the south west corner follow the bank for about 250 yards. At a point where the trees rise to the edge of the camp, take the footpath on the left (not very clearly defined).

The path fish-hooks back to drop diagonally left down the steep hillside to meet a stile hidden beneath the overhanging branches of a large tree. Follow the path through a short stretch of trees to meet a crossing path by a rock outcrop. Here turn right and in a few yards, at a further junction turn left down a hollow way to meet the road at Hydegate.

Join the lane signposted to Cam and in a little over 100 yards take the bridleway on the right, heading in the direction of Peaked Down. The way is between thick hedges.

Ignore the first turn to the left and the subsequent crossing. Maintain your northwesterly direction for about 700 yards after leaving the road at Hydegate. Here, disregard the track to the right and bear left a little to join the signed bridleway.

The path curves slowly to the left and in about 300 yards enters a wood via a metal gate. Continue with a broad track, which can be very churned up. You may prefer to find the slightly higher path that seems to have developed as a result and runs through bracken.

Ahead see the path descending from Peaked Down, which is reached about 200 yards after entering the wooded area. Here fish-hook right, taking care to find the waymarked Cotswold Way (white spot) and follow this northeasterly to the summit of Cam Long Down. (If in any doubt, move forward to the little clearing where several paths meet at the foot of Peaked Down. You should have no difficulty in selecting the right one). The bracken edged path climbs to the summit and another excellent viewpoint.

> This walk has been one of ups and downs but there is always a reward for effort. Downham Hill and Uley Bury are seen across the valley with Frocester Hill towards the north.

At the eastern end of the summit, the Cotswold Way is waymarked running steeply downhill to the right. After passing through a short wooded area it emerges into open fields and descends to meet a lane by farm buildings. Keep with the lane for about 200 yards, as it bends to the right bear left towards Hodgecombe Farm. A signpost is shortly seen indicating Uley Bury and Frocester Hill.

Remain with this track which leads towards Hodgecombe Farm. A mail box for the farm has the direction painted on it. Just beyond the farm take the narrow path directly ahead which plunges into a wood, climbs, widens and becomes a deep, dark hollow way.

As the road is reached near the summit, turn left on a narrow path. This terraces the hillside under beech trees, with views of Cam Long Down and the River Severn beyond. The sheer face of an old quarry reveals the whiteness of the limestone in this part of the Cotswolds. The man-made cliff is a fresh habitat for birds.

After a long stretch of level walking the path is stepped downhill. Continue over a crossing path and, at a junction by a cottage, turn right on a wide track to climb again. After a long steep pull through the woods emerge at a road and turn left.

At the next road junction there is a small wooden cross — placed here it may be supposed after another tragic road accident.

Take the road fork to the left and after a short distance join the path on the right. This passes through a wooded section again with old quarry faces. On leaving the trees, the path follows the edge of Frocester Hill, yet another fine viewpoint, the last of the day.

Here, you may turn to look back to Downham Hill, Cam Long Down and the tall finger of the Tyndale memorial. The wide silvery Severn, perhaps tinged with pink slowly deepening to blood red as the sun sets, a colourful contrast to the black silhouetted towers of Berkeley Power Station. Overhead the silent craft of the nearby Gloucester and Bristol Gliding Club soar like great prehistoric birds towards the vale below.

A topograph identifies a clutch of distant points, including the Malvern Hills 24 miles, Gloucester 11 miles, the Black Mountains 40 miles, Brecon Beacons 50 miles and the Severn Railway Bridge 7½ miles. Alas this is no longer true, for the bridge was badly damaged in 1960 when struck by an oil barge. A further collision led to the closure of the line and the dismantling of the bridge. The tower on the eastern side remains as a memorial to what was once the longest bridge in England.

Walk 15: The Battle, The Bible and The Bride

Nibley Knoll and Wotton-under-Edge

Route: North Nibley — Nibley Knoll — Wotton Hill — Wotton-under-Edge — Holywell — Coombe Hill (edge) — Westridge Wood — Nibley Knoll — North Nibley

Map: 1:50,000 Landranger Sheet 162, 1:25,000 Pathfinder 1132 (ST69/79)

Distance: 5½ miles

Parking: Small layby, edge of North Nibley B4060 near cemetery

Toilets: Wotton-under-Edge

North Nibley doesn't quite have the ring of history about its name, but here two contrasting events are recalled. The first dates back to 1470. The private armies of Viscount Lisle and Lord Berkeley met at Nibley Green to decide, by force of arms, the long-running dispute over the ownership of Berkeley Castle and the great estates. At one time it was said that you couldn't walk to London from Gloucestershire without crossing Berkeley land for most of the way. The battle resulted in the death of both contenders. The second is the reason for the tall column set on the hill above the village.

The walk starts from the layby beneath Nibley Knoll and its memorial tower honouring the memory of William Tyndale. It is possible to climb to the top of the monument but only if you are in possession of the key. This can be collected from the village shop in Barrs Lane at the following times: Monday to Saturday 9-5 except Wednesday 9-12. Other arrangements exist; for up to date details please consult the notice board close to the point where the Cotswold Way leaves the road.

The Walk

From the layby walk towards the village for a short distance to join the Cotswold Way signposted on the right. There are two possible routes to the summit. The first is the now-restored original route, which soon leads off on the right climbing steeply the way now eased by steps. An easier progress is made by maintaining your direction through the woods. As the top of the hill is neared, leave the main path and turn to the right. After a short passage under trees, reach a stile and bear half right to the Tyndale monument.

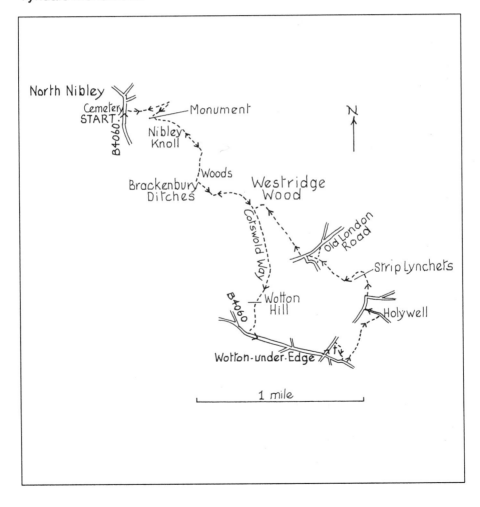

Tyndale Monument on Nibley Knoll

Whether or not you climb the steps to the top of the 111-feet high tower, you are again presented with an excellent viewpoint.

To the north is Stinchcombe Hill. The clear patch on the top accommodates a golf course. To the west the wooded hillside falls steeply to the Severn plain, beyond the river lies the once remote Forest of Dean. Behind to the east is Ozleworth Tower, while downstream are the great towers of the Severn Bridge. Again we are assisted by a topograph, calling our attention to Lansdowne Hill 780 feet, 17 miles just to the east of south, and Abergavenny's distinctive Sugar Loaf Mountain, 33 miles distant. Haresfield Beacon is found 10 miles to the northeast. Nearer is Berkeley Castle with a long history, which includes the horrific murder of Edward II in its stinking dungeons.

William Tyndale was a Gloucestershire man, born only a few years after the arrival of the printing press. Caxton's revolutionary invention was to education what the wheel was to transport. Tyndale's stated aim was to provide a bible that would be available to all, to be read or heard in the language of the people. He took a post as tutor to the family of Sir John Walsh in Little Sodbury and settled down to his work of translating the New Testament. Lack of patronage and active opposition led to his departure to the continent where he completed the translation. The book was already partly printed when the Cologne authorities prevented the printer from completing the work and Tyndale was obliged to move on.

In 1526, when copies of the book reached England from Worms, the Bishop of London had the book burnt publicly at St. Paul's Cross. Tyndale never returned to his native land, his powerful opponents in England included the equally ill-fated Sir Thomas More. Tyndale was seized in Antwerp and carried off to Brussels where he was burnt at the stake in 1536.

Three hundred and thirty years later Tyndale, a prophet without honour in his own country, was handsomely commemorated by the tower that now dominates the landscape. The inscription is brief:

"Erected AD 1866, in grateful remembrance of William Tyndale, translator of the English Bible, he first caused the New Testament to be printed in the mother tongue of his countrymen. Born near this spot he suffered martyrdom at Vilvorde in Flanders on Oct 6 1536."

Continue with the Cotswold Way, following the fence along the edge of the hill towards the woods. A broad track runs through the wood, passing, but hidden from sight by the trees, Brackenbury Ditches, another hill fort.

After about half a mile the path runs between the wood on the right and cultivated land to the left. At the edge of the wood, by a Fire Danger sign, the path bears off half right to follow the edge of an open field with a thick hedge to the right. At the end of this long rectangular field, take the path off half right by an almost hidden stile. Go forward to a clump of fir trees, surrounded by a wall and seats. This is a favoured local view point

Below lies Wotton-under-Edge, located as its name suggests beneath the steep Cotswold escarpment. The trees featured here were first planted in 1815 to commemorate Wellington's victory at Waterloo. The inscription records that when the Crimean War was being celebrated the trees were felled and used for a bonfire. They like their bonfires in this part of the world and contributed to the chain of beacons that spanned the country at Queen Victoria's Jubilee in 1887. Trees were then replanted and the encircling wall erected. The present trees date from 1952.

From the celebratory clump of pines, go forward taking the path that runs downhill towards Wotton. After about 100 yards, cross a stile to meet metalled lane. Take the path opposite, which is followed to meet a road. Here turn left to meet the edge of the town. Turn left descending Bradley Road, which leads on to Gloucester Street to reach Old Town. There is at least one house with a fake window painted in, a more than symbolic device to shut the tax man out. The window tax was replaced in 1851 by a tax on the house itself — an enlightened reform?

Wotton-under-Edge is another in the scatter of wool towns around the Cotswold Hills. Among its famous 'old boys' is Edward Jenner, whose pioneering work from 1796, in the use of vaccine for the prevention of small pox, would, in today's world, have won him a Nobel Prize.

An invention that had a substantial impact on the commercial and journalistic world was the introduction of Stenographic Soundhand in 1837. If that sounds less than familiar then there will be no difficulty with its more common name, Pitman's Shorthand. Sir Isaac, as he became, was a local schoolmaster and lived in Orchard Street. His work on outlines, diphthongs, phrases and vowel signs was to spread across the world, a revolution in the recording and reporting of the spoken word.

St. Mary's Church, a prominent landmark from our Wotton Hill view point, is on our way and should be visited. A former vicar, Dr. Tattersall, brought off something of a coup at the end of the eighteenth century. He bought a second hand organ. No big deal on the face of it, worth only a paragraph in the local paper except, that is, for the antecedents of the instrument.

George I had held the office of church warden at the recently completed, and now famous, St. Martin's in the Fields, in London. On retiring from that position after only a short period he provided the church with a handsome new organ, at a cost of fifteen hundred guineas. It was suitably launched on its musical career by George Frederick Handel, no less, but not with the Hallelujah Chorus, it had yet to be written. In 1799 the church authorities decided to replace the organ and having done so had the embarrassing problem of disposing of the king's gift. Wotton's vicar snapped it up for £200. It must have been worth that for the inscription alone which reads "Gift of his most sacred Majesty King George 1726."

The Berkeley family connection with the church is strong. Catherine, Lady Berkeley, shortly before her death in 1385 founded the Wotton Grammar School and the Chantry Chapel.

The tenth Earl of Berkeley (1352-1417) was known as Thomas the Magnificent. Certainly, he and his wife Margaret (a daughter of Lord Lisle) are magnificently remembered in the fine brasses on their tombs.

Thomas succeeded to the title in 1368, his father Maurice the Valiant having succumbed to wounds sustained at the Battle of Poitiers. The previous year, Thomas, being only 14, had married

Margaret and if that sounds a trifle young, his bride was only half his age. 'Marriage of convenience' is a phrase that comes immediately to mind. However, they seem to have achieved such a good relationship that when she died at the early age of 31 he never remarried, although he survived her for a quarter of a century. The (missing) inscription from the tomb sums up his faithfulness even beyond death – we are told it read:

"In youth our parents joined our hands, ourselves our hearts,
In this tombe our bodyes, hath the heaven our better parts."

They had only one child, a daughter, Elizabeth, it was this lack of male issue that led to the problems over the ownership of Berkeley.

From the churchyard, go south through the wrought iron gates to reach the road. Here turn left and after crossing a small bridge turn left to follow the fast flowing stream, which once turned the mills of Wotton. Ignore the first little arched bridge. Thereafter the route crosses and recrosses the water, and in a little under half a mile reaches Holywell at a junction with a narrow lane. Turn left, climbing Holywell Lane to turn right at a T-junction.

When the road bends, at the foot of a 1-in-10 hill, take the track on the left. After a few yards, cross a stile to climb the steep slopes of Coombe Hill. Across the southern slopes run the strip lynchets of earlier farming. When a crossing track is reached turn left terracing the hillside with views of Wotton and the little hamlet of Holywell.

As the path enters a beech wood there are views to Conygre Wood opposite. As the summit is reached, a further track is joined; turn left with this and after about 200 yards bear left on a path between wire fencing. After 150 yards this meets the Old London Road, turn left and in a few yards take the broad track on the right signed to Tyndale Monument. There is cultivated land to the left and woodland on the right fringed with brambles.

When the large field meets the wood, turn left on the path following the inside edge of the wood to join the Cotswold Way, which is met in 150 yards. Turn right and keep with the waymarked path to make a return through the woods to emerge with the tall finger of Tyndale's monument seen ahead.

From here, retrace your steps to North Nibley.

Last Steps

I call this Last Steps only because it is the last chapter (apart from the useful information section that follows) in this book. There are no last steps for the walker until the time comes for him to hang up his boots. When we left the Cotswold Way at Wotton-under-Edge, it still had nearly thirty miles to run before knocking at the west door of Bath Abbey.

The walks described have covered rather more distance than the Cotswold Way itself. We have seen the seasons change from spring to the onset of autumn, watched the wild flowers of the hedgerow bloom, drop their seed and fade away. The crops planted by man have come to maturity and been harvested and the plough is again at work. On the hilltops we have had an inkling of how our prehistoric ancestors tilled the land and tended their flocks, perhaps more civilised communities than we believed. In the towns and villages we have seen how the animal husbandry of the early farmers grew into a great weaving industry.

We have seen a little of the tidal flow of history, the rise and fall of people, the good, the bad and the ugly. The remains of ancient castles and abbey ruins have had something to say of the good times and the bad times, of war and famine, of peace and prosperity. Although fate, fickle mistress that she is, sometimes decreed a reversal of these roles, with war bringing prosperity for some and peace not always walking hand in hand with plenty.

The field paths and bridleways that we have followed for pleasure were once part of the communications network of the country and are as much a part of our national heritage as our stately homes or great cathedrals. They are equally to be preserved and respected, a responsibility to be shared by landowners, farmers, walkers and government both local and national.

This book has concerned itself mainly with the small towns and villages. May I recommend that if you have not yet had the pleasure of a visit to Bath, you complete your exploration of the Cotswold ways by spending a day in that exceptionally fine city?

Pulteney Bridge over the River Avon, Bath

Useful Information

Tourist Information Offices

(Note – some offices are seasonal opening)
Bath: 11-13 Bath Street, Tel: 01225 462831
Broadway: 1 Cotswold Court, Tel: 01386 852937
Cheltenham: 77 Promenade, Tel: 01242 522878
Chipping Campden: Woolstaplers Hall High St, Tel: 01386 840101
Gloucester: St. Michael's Tower, The Cross, Tel: 01452 421188
Painswick: The Library, Stroud Road, Tel: 01452 813552
Stroud: George Street, Tel: 01453 765768
Winchcombe: Town Hall, High Street, Tel: 01242 602925

Maps

The complete list of 1:50,000 Landranger Sheets required for the suggested walks is given below with relevant walk numbers.

150 – Worcester and the Malverns	1, 2, 3, 4, 5 and part of 6
151 – Stratford-on-Avon	part of 1
162 – Gloucester & Forest of Dean	12, 13, 14 and 15
163 – Cheltenham & Cirencester	6, 7, 8, 9, 10, 11

Note: Sheet 172 overlaps very slightly with 162 and is required if further exploration south of Wotton-under-edge to Bath is undertaken.

The greater detail afforded by the 1:25,000 Pathfinder sheets is very welcome but represents a larger investment. The appropriate sheets are indicated in the relevant chapter headings.

Accommodation

Accommodation of all kinds is available throughout the length of the Cotswold Way. For latest information contact the appropriate

Tourist Information Office or consult The Cotswold Way Handbook published annually and available locally or by post from the Ramblers Association 1-5 Wandsworth Road, London SW8 2LJ.

Travel

Nearest British Rail stations: Moreton-in-Marsh, Evesham, Cheltenham, Gloucester, Bath. A number of bus services operate in the area. The Cotswold Way Handbook provides an updated list with telephone numbers for enquiries.

Places of Interest On or Near the Walks

Times and seasons quoted are for guidance only and may be subject to variation. If making a special visit, check with establishment, local advertising or the nearest Tourist Information Office. The listing is roughly in the order of the walks – those directly on the route are marked with a *.

Hidcote Manor Garden *(National Trust)*

4 miles from Chipping Campden; April to October from 11 a.m., not Tuesday or Friday.

* Woolstaplers Hall Museum

Chipping Campden; April to September and October, weekends from 11 a.m.

* St. Eadburgha's Church

Broadway; April to end-September

* Broadway Country Park

Nature trail, animals, birds, exhibition in tower; April to end-September or early October

* Snowshill Manor & The Charles Wade Collection *(National Trust)*

Easter to October, afternoons (not Tuesday)

Hidcote Manor Gardens

* Stanton church

Daily

* Stanway House

Tuesday and Thursday afternoons, June to September.

GWR Steam Railway

Toddington; Sunday, late March to late October; Bank Holidays and some Saturdays and Wednesdays during the holiday season

* Hailes Abbey *(English Heritage/NT)*

Daily from 9.30 a.m.

* Sudeley Castle

House, garden and various attractions and events; daily, April to October

* Winchcombe

Railway Museum 23 Gloucester St.; Afternoons daily

Sims Police Museum & Folk Museum

Town Hall; March to October, Monday to Saturday, from 10 a.m. Church; daily

* Belas Knap long barrow

Any time

Tewkesbury

Historic town and superb abbey, Battlefield trail, Town Museum and John Moore Museum of the Countryside

Cotswold Farm Park

Rare breeds centre, nr Guiting Power; Daily, Easter to October

Cheltenham

Regency Spa Town, Pump Room, Gallery of Fashion, Art Gallery, Museum, excellent shopping.

Crickley Hill Country Park
Daily

Gloucester
Historic city, Cathedral, Restored Docks with National Inland Waterways Museum, Museum of Advertising and Packing, Antique Centre. Excellent folk museum.

* Prinknash Abbey
Pottery, Shop, viewing gallery etc.; Daily.

* Painswick Church
Daily

Slimbridge Wild Fowl & Wetlands Trust
Daily from 9.30 a.m.

Westonbirt Arboretum
Daily

Berkeley Castle
Tues to Sun, April to September, 2-5 p.m.; Sunday only in October. Jenner museum close by and interesting church

Viewpoints

(some may require a walk from car park)
Dovers Hill near Chipping Campden
Broadway Hill (park at Fish Hill picnic site or from Country park)
Cleeve Hill (walk from car park)
Leckhampton Hill (walk from Daisy Bank car park)
Crickley Hill Country Park
Barrow Wake (signed from A417)
Shortwood Topograph (short walk)
Haresfield Beacon (short walk)
Coaley Peak Country Park
Tyndale Monument (steep climb from North Nibley)